RUN RIVER RUN

For my brother Ian and the inspiration we shared.

RUN RIVER RUN

CANOEING BRITAIN'S FINEST RIVERS

A Topographic Guide by Alan Fox

DIADEM BOOKS · LONDON
1990

Published in 1990 by Diadem Books Limited, London

British Library and Cataloguing Data available
ISBN 0-906371-77-5

Trade enquiries to Hodder & Stoughton Ltd.,
Mill Road, Dunton Green, Sevenoaks, Kent TN13 2YA

Printed in Great Britain by BPCC Hazell Books Ltd.,
Aylesbury and Arkle Print, Northampton

ACKNOWLEDGEMENTS I would like to thank the many
people who have in some way, however small, contributed to
this book with advice, information, criticism but above all with
enthusiasm.
    In particular: Graham Mackereth for the initial concept and
Ken Wilson for developing the idea, Len Smith for advice on
the River Tees, Kevin Chamberlain for advice on the River Dart,
Clive Freshwater for advice on the River Spey, David Hope
for advice on the River Usk, the Measllwch Arms Canoe Centre
for advice on the River Wye, George Davis for advice on the
Afon Tryweryn, Roger Haywood for advice on the River Dee,
Jerry Tracey and Haefen Adventure for advice on the North-
East rivers and to numerous individuals for general advice:
Stuart Fisher, Colin Butler, Ray Rowe, Colin Kempson, Ken
Vickers, Colin Broadway, Mike Twiggs, Carel Quaife and the
River Advisers of the British Canoe Union, The Welsh Canoe
Association and the Scottish Canoe Association. For photo-
graphic assistance I am indebted to: Chris Dickinson, Antony
Glanville and Paul Moore for their pictures used in the book
and also to Ross Purdy, Les Lloyd, Kevin Chamberlain and
Colin Butler.
    Finally my thanks to all those people who have kept me
'afloat' over the years, and in particular Anne Garland for
keeping me relatively sane during the compilation of this
guide.

CONTENTS

Photographs in the Text

Rivers Tees, Lune, Eden, Findhorn, Spey and Orchy   *between pages* 32/33

Rivers Marteg, Usk, Wye, Dee, Tryweryn, Llugwy and Conwy   *between pages* 96/97

All photos are from the author's archive except 6 (Antony Glanville), 7, 8 and 11 (Chris Dickinson) 12 and 17 (Paul Moore). The cover photo shows the author on the River Etive.

General Location Maps in the Text

Notes on the Maps and Descriptions

The book is designed for use on the river. The guidebook narratives are broken up into convenient paragraphs that describe logical sections of river, each paragraph starting with an obvious landmark.

The detailed maps are drawn to a large scale each covering a stretch of river – usually a stage in the narrative. The maps are organised so that rivers flow from the top to bottom of the page regardless of the north orientation and river widths are exaggerated for the greater clarity of small details.

All maps noted in the headings refer to the Ordnance Survey 1.50,000 Landranger Series.

 Road.

------- Footpath.

 Contours, crags.

• 301   Spot height.

Footbridge.
Ropeway
Steep bank
Rocky bank / Gorge

Rapids : grade 1 - 2.

Rapids : grade 2 - 3.

Rapids: grade 3 - 5.
Caution / Hazard.
Fall / Weir – portage route.

INTRODUCTION

Rocky outcrops towered above the dense green vegetation that clung precariously to the valley sides. The impenetrable darkness of the forest skirted the banks and kept the river on its course of wide and graceful meanders. Ahead lay the rapid, the crescendo of its roar enveloping the surroundings as we paddled closer towards it. Fear and uncertainty gripped my stomach, and for the first time in my life I wondered what I had let myself in for.

'Paddle Hard' was the order of the day but my limbs felt weak and heavy, reluctant, like my mind, to commit itself to the torrent ahead. The river made the decision for me, sweeping the canoe downstream, leaving no time for hesitation or doubt. I reached forward and dug the paddle blade deep into the water and pulled hard. Waves crashed down on the foredeck, the canoe rocked up and down and the spray blinded my eyes. My heart was still leaping but I continued to paddle hard, and slowly my fear began to dissolve as I realised that I could actually control my canoe in the fast water. Suddenly it was all over and I had reached the calm water. My fear had turned to elation and I had become addicted to canoeing, but more importantly I had survived my first descent of Symonds Yat rapids.

From the first canoeing experience a whole new world was opened up to me, a world of exploration, adventure and excitement. Every new river trip became a journey into the unknown and every river had its own distinct personality. As my skills developed, my thirst for different rivers increased: Scotland, North Wales, Northern England, the European Alps, and further afield to rivers that I had seen only as a thin blue line on a map yet which held the promise of adventure. Canoeing became an incentive to visit new places, meet new people and form lasting friendships and at the same time it provided an escape from the routine of work and the frantic pace of everyday life. I found that it could embrace all my moods, from quiet meditative and tranquil drifting to the wild and turbulent descents where decisions are critical and life becomes precious. At the end of the day it doesn't matter whether the river is wild or calm, what matters most of all is being there.

The river environment has so much to offer; there is something for everyone, for the fisherman, the pleasure boater, the naturalist and the walker. These rivers are our natural heritage and it is our responsibility as a nation and as individuals to preserve them as such and to share them so that everyone may benefit equally from their refreshing spirit.

Canoeing is perhaps the best way of exploring these rivers for the canoe is environmentally acceptable, there is no pollution or damage from the ripple of its wake and its passing does little or nothing to disturb the eco-system of the river. The rivers in this guide are some of the most popular canoeing rivers in Britain, but this selection is by no means definitive or exhaustive, for everyone will have their own favourite stretch of water. The guides and maps are written to give an overview of what each river has to offer. It is then up to you to explore them further, to organise your own adventures on the water and to discover for yourselves the experience of 'being there'.

GENERAL INFORMATION

Getting Started

If you are new to canoeing then the best ways to start are either to join a canoe club or attend a course or activity holiday. This should enable you to learn the basic techniques involved, try out different types of canoes and equipment and to find out how much more the sport of canoeing has to offer. Details of local canoe clubs, courses and activity centres can be obtained from the governing bodies of canoeing in England, Wales, Scotland and Northern Ireland.

The British Canoe Union

The British Canoe Union, formed in 1936, is canoeing's national organisation with over 700 affiliated clubs. Its purpose is to unite everyone interested in canoeing and encourage others to join in. It aims to provide a complete service to paddlers – education, information, improved access to canoeable waters, and increasing the enjoyment, safety and skills of all paddlers at every level. The BCU is affiliated to the International Canoe Federation and the Olympic Association and is responsible for national and international competition.

The responsibility for canoeing in Scotland, Wales and Northern Ireland has been delegated to the relevant national associations: the Scottish Canoe Association, the Welsh Canoe Association and the Northern Ireland Canoe Association. Canoeing in England is administered by the BCU.

Membership of your relevant canoe association can provide you with inclusive, comprehensive insurance covering life, accident, canoes and third party liability, free canal and river licences, a regular colour magazine *Canoe Focus*, local river and coastal information, skills courses and coaching, proficiency tests and free advice and help on any aspect of canoeing. The members' Year Book gives details of all events and courses.

Access

Any access points indicated on the maps within this guide do not necessarily imply a right of access, especially across private land where permission should be obtained beforehand. Access to the river may be from three points:

- Where a place to which the public have access joins the river, i.e. a road or bridge. • Across private land where access has been agreed. • From tidal water.

Access Considerations in England and Wales

Under English law many non-tidal waters are privately owned and the owners may or may not give permission for canoeing. Some larger rivers are public navigations, though sometimes requiring the payment of tolls. In seeking access to private waters conflict can arise between canoeing and angling interests. Where conflict has arisen the National Canoeing Associations of England and Wales, the British Canoe Union (BCU) and the Welsh Canoe Association (WCA), through its regional and local Access Officers, work to achieve access agreements in co-operation with the Riparian Owners and Angling Associations, that secure fair and reasonable access for canoeists.

Details of access agreements and a list of Access Officers are available from the relevant national association. All access agreements must be strictly adhered to in order not to jeopardise access for others or access in the future. Access agreements can change, and advice should be sought in advance from the Access Officer for the river.

Where no access agreement exists permission should be sought from the Riparian Owners for access to the river and along it. Unauthorised access to private waters may constitute an act of trespass. If challenged by the Riparian Owner or an agent for the owner you may be asked to leave the river, in which case you must do so by the route agreed with by the challenger. Act politely and considerately at all times.

In the long term the BCU and WCA are working to achieve a situation where canoeists can paddle all waters suitable for canoeing without challenge, but with reasonable consideration for other water users and with due regard for the law and the conservation of the environment in line with the principles of the Council of Europe's Charter 'Sport for All'.

Access Considerations for Scotland
The law in Scotland is somewhat different from that in England. Consequently the problems faced by paddlers in Scotland are very different from those faced in England and Wales.

The Scottish Canoe Association (SCA), which is the governing body for canoeing in Scotland, asks all paddlers to be polite and considerate to other water users, believing strongly in 'Sport for All'. The SCA is not party to any access agreements in Scotland. Some clubs do have local agreements and so the position on access in any area should be checked by contacting the SCA in advance.

Current Access Situations
Access agreements exist in some form, whether written or verbal, on all the rivers in England and Wales described in this guide, as well as on many other rivers. Access agreements can change and it is therefore in your own interests and in the interests of canoeing in general that you make prior contact with the Local or Regional Access Officers for the river in question. The Access Officers work voluntarily in securing agreements for canoeing, and will also be able to give details of current river conditions and other important local information.

Note: The names and addresses of Access Officers frequently change and are best obtained from the relevant National Canoeing Association.

USEFUL ADDRESSES
British Canoe Union (BCU)   Adbolton Lane, West Bridgford, Nottingham NG2 5AF ☎ 0602 691944

Scottish Canoe Association (SCA) Caledonian House, South Gyle, Edinburgh EH12 9DQ ☎ 031 3177314

Welsh Canoe Association (WCA) The Whitewater Centre, Canolfan Tryweryn, Bala, Gwynedd LL23 7NU ☎ 0678 520826

Canoe Association of Northern Ireland House of Sport, Upper Malone Road, Belfast, N. Ireland BT9 5LA ☎ 0232 381222

WEIL'S DISEASE
an important health warning

All watersports carry the risk of infection from Weil's Disease. However, the incidence of occurrence in canoeing has been very small. The following notes have been reproduced by kind permission of the British Canoe Union, who advise anyone suffering from the symptoms outlined below to consult their doctor as soon as possible and to show him the information below in case there is any doubt in his diagnosis.

What is it? Weil's Disease is a bacterial infection carried in rats' urine which contaminates water and wet river banks. The bacteria does not survive for long in dry conditions. The risk of infection is greater where stagnant or slow-moving water is involved, but cases have occurred on swift-moving streams as well as lowland rivers.

How serious is it? It can be a serious illness requiring hospital treatment and can lead to kidney or liver failure. One patient in nineteen dies with it. Weil's Disease is a notifiable illness.

How do I catch it? The bacteria are absorbed through the skin and mucous membranes of the mouth and eyes. It gets into the bloodstream more easily if you have a minor cut on your skin or feet or if you do capsize drill or rolling.

What should I do about it? If you feel ill after canoeing, particularly from 3 to 19 days following, then see your doctor IMMEDIATELY. The most common early symptoms are: temperature, an influenza-like illness, and joint and muscle pains. (Pains in the calf muscles are often particularly noticeable.) Jaundice and/or conjunctivitis may be present, or develop, although the absence of any of these symptoms does not mean that the illness is not Weil's Disease – nor does a symptom in isolation necessarily indicate that Weil's Disease is present.

Tell your doctor you have been canoeing and where and ask if you can have a blood test for Weil's Disease. Tell the BCU who will let their medical panel know about it.

In Summary
- Avoid capsize drill or rolling in stagnant or slow-moving water.
- Wash or shower after canoeing.
- Cover minor scratches on exposed parts of the body with waterproof plaster.
- Use foot-wear to avoid cutting feet.
- If you have flu-like illness after canoeing go to your GP early – tell him you are a canoeist.

Early identification of the illness is vital

Your doctor is reminded of the existence of:
The Leptospirosis Reference Unit, Public Health Laboratory, County Hospital, Hereford HR1 2ER

Important Note on the Treatment of Weil's Disease
Results of blood tests have been known to take 2 – 3 weeks through the normal laboratory system. Watersports persons have become seriously ill, and some have even died, through slow diagnosis and treatment. The local public health laboratory should be equipped to undertake an ELISA test, from which a result can be obtained within 3 hours of commencement. Otherwise the sample should be sent to the Leptospirosis Reference Unit at Hereford.

The BCU issues each member with a pink card carrying details about Weil's Disease.

A NOTE ON RIVER SAFETY

The descriptions in this guide are intended to give an overall impression of what each river has to offer the canoeist. A rock-by-rock approach has been avoided due to the ever-changing nature of the river environment. Fallen trees, rock slides, floods and droughts can change the course of the river and alter individual rapids and the changing water levels will affect the grading of the river. Other factors that may influence your river trip are: the prevailing weather conditions, the number of canoeists in a group and their ability, and the amount of available daylight.

In all cases it is the responsibility of the individual or the group leader to assess the situation, check local conditions and to make the appropriate decisions in organising the canoeing trip in the day. The use of *common sense* cannot be stressed enough!

Ten Useful Safety Tips

1. Learn to canoe properly and safely, if necessary take a course of instruction.
2. Wear an approved buoyancy aid or life jacket and use recommended equipment.
3. Check prevailing weather conditions and river levels and allow adequate time to complete your trip.
4. Do not canoe alone, but if you must, let someone know where you are going and your estimated time of arrival.
5. If you have not canoed before or you are uncertain about a particular river, then ask someone with experience to accompany you.
6. Be aware of hazards on the rivers, in particular: overhanging or submerged trees, weirs (inspect and portage if in doubt), moored craft, pleasure cruisers and rowing sculls.
7. Respect the environment and other water users. Keep clear of anglers and their lines, pass through fishing pools quickly and quietly. Do not disturb areas important for wintering wildfowl, nesting birds and spawning fish.
8. Learn first aid and resuscitation techniques.
9. Do not canoe and drink alcohol.
10. Have fun safely!

GRADINGS

The gradings used in this guide are as follows:

Grade 1. Easy – moving water with occasional small rapids, few or no obstacles.

Grade 2. Medium – small rapids but easy to navigate with regular waves.

Grade 3. Difficult – rapids with irregular waves and hazards that need avoiding. Complex manoeuvring often required and inspection may be needed.

Grade 4. Very Difficult – large rapids and falls, precise manoeuvring required, dangerous hydraulics and hazards. Inspection necessary and rescue difficult. Rolling ability often needed.

Grade 5. Extremely Difficult – complex and difficult rapids with dangerous hydraulics and difficult route-finding. Inspection essential. Rolling ability essential. Rescue difficult or impossible. Hazard to life.

Grade 6. Limit of Navigation – Grade 5 carried to the extreme of navigation, nearly impossible. A fine line between success or failure. It is better to spectate!

Note: The grading of a river may change according to the river levels. The gradings given are for favourable conditions.

DISCLAIMER

The information in this guidebook relates to where it is physically possible to canoe and does not imply a legal right to canoe the rivers mentioned or a right of access to the rivers.

For updated information on access to the rivers in England, Wales and Scotland contact should be made in advance with the relevant Access Officers of the British Canoe Union, the Welsh Canoe Association and the Scottish Canoe Associaton.

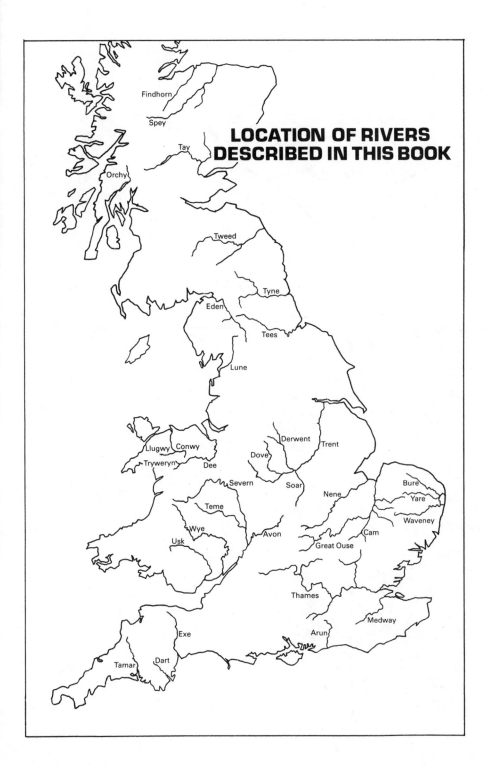

LOCATION OF RIVERS DESCRIBED IN THIS BOOK

Findhorn

Spey

Tay

Orchy

Tweed

Tyne

Eden

Tees

Lune

Llugwy   Conwy

Tryweryn

Dee

Derwent   Trent

Dove

Severn   Soar

Nene

Bure

Yare

Waveney

Teme

Wye

Avon

Cam

Usk

Great Ouse

Thames

Medway

Exe

Arun

Tamar   Dart

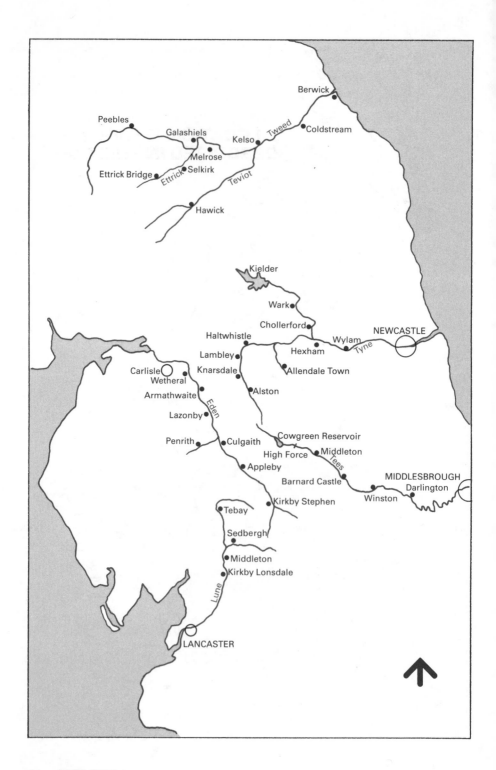

RIVER TYNE

ALSTON TO WYLAM

OS Sheets 87/88   48 miles/77km   Grade 2

The Tyne river system offers a great deal of good canoeing in very attractive and largely unspoilt rural surroundings. The Tyne has two major branches: the North Tyne and the South Tyne which converge near the market town of Hexham.

The South Tyne has its source high on the fells of Alston Moor only a few miles to the east of where the River Tees originates. From Alston, England's highest market town, the river flows through a green and wooded valley with the high moors rising on either side. At Haltwhistle it curves eastward. A major tributary, the River Allen, joins before Haydon Bridge and just before Hexham the North Tyne converges to swell the flow, and the combined rivers now become the Tyne.

The North Tyne is fed by the many streams of the Kielder Forest. In 1982 the Kielder Dam was opened, creating a vast reservoir for watersports and fishing.

From Hexham the Tyne continues its eastward journey until it becomes tidal at Wylam and from here the banks are built up and industrialised until it reaches the sea at Tynemouth.

The upper reaches of the Tyne and its tributaries provide spate runs of interest to whitewater paddlers. Further downstream there are many stretches ideal for touring and training at a range of standards. The rapids, for the most part, consist of boulder fields rather than bedrock channels and this gives an 'open' character to the river, but route finding can at times be a problem. There is a tendency towards shallowness at low water but high water, however, produces good 'big water' conditions at many places instead of causing a washing-out effect. Conditions are at their best after rain, but interesting and enjoyable water can be found somewhere within the catchment area in all but the very driest of weather periods.

Parties interested in guided river descents, coaching or instruction in this area, or accommodation during visits, should contact 'Haefen Adventure', Haefen House, Middle Hay Leazes, Allendale, NE47 9NP (☎ 043483 409).

Access consideration for the River Tyne

No right of navigation exists on the Tyne upstream of the tidal limit at Wylam though a good understanding exists between the riparian owners and local canoeists. It is hoped that visiting canoeists will help promote this co-operation by behaving reasonably and by showing courtesy to other water users. Favourable access agreements exist for the whole Tyne catchment area and up-to-date information is available from the Regional Access Officer (BCU).

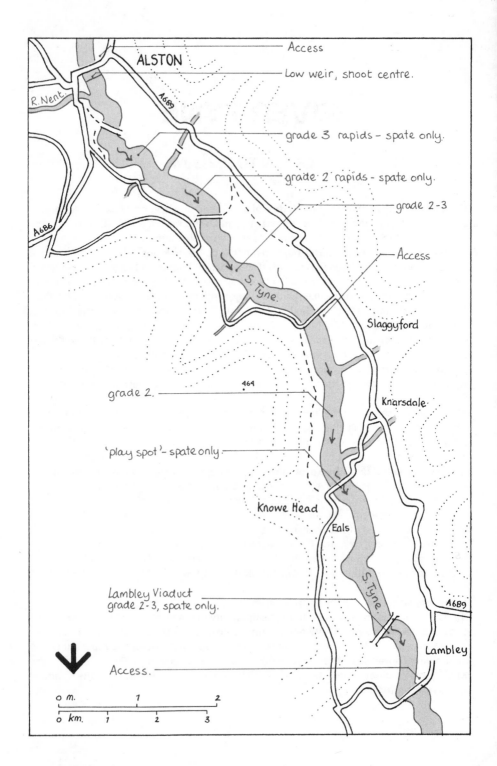

Access
ALSTON
Low weir, shoot centre.
R. Nent
A686
grade 3 rapids – spate only.
grade 2 rapids – spate only.
grade 2-3
Access
A686
S. Tyne.
Slaggyford
grade 2.
464
Knarsdale
'play spot' – spate only
Knowe Head
Eals
Lambley Viaduct
grade 2-3, spate only.
S. Tyne.
A689
Lambley
Access.

0 m.   1   2
0 km.   1   2   3

Alston to Haltwhistle

*Start (716461)   Finish (700634)   Grade 2 – 3 (spate only)   Distance 16mls/24km
(Alston Bridge to Slaggyford Bridge 5mls/8km   Slaggyford Bridge to Lambley Bridge 7mls/10km
Lambley Bridge to Haltwhistle 4mls/6km)*

The run from Alston down to Lambley is only feasible in high water conditions. It is then an excellent Grade 2 – 3 run with many sections of sustained fast and powerful rapids. In any lower conditions it will prove to be too shallow and rocky and therefore not worthwhile. Fallen trees often constitute a major hazard on this upper section. Access at Alston is upstream of the bridge (716461) on the left-hand side. A low weir beyond this is shot in the centre, though it is washed out in spate conditions. At such times there are a combination of fast Grade 2 and Grade 3 rapids. Care should be taken at Slaggyford Bridge (681519) where the water is fast and powerful.

Downstream from Slaggyford the river becomes more open with continuous Grade 2 rapids and the occasional Grade 3. At Knowe Head (682553) there is a good playspot in the stoppers below the bridge and at Lambley Viaduct a Grade 3 rapid follows with a long section of exploding waves.

At Lambley Bridge (676596) there is access on the left bank immediately upstream of the bridge. Below the bridge the river is Grade 1 – 2 with fallen trees being an additional problem. Featherstone Castle is passed on the right and beyond this is Featherstone Weir which can be shot on the right in medium to low levels, though it is best to portage right in spate. The next section to Bridge End (676618) is a good Grade 2, useful for training, and the road on the right gives easy access and a walk-back for multiple runs and a good vantage for coaching. From this point the river is now more canoeable in medium water levels being generally Grade 2 down to Haltwhistle where there is a good exit/access point on the right bank after the first bridge (700634).

Haltwhistle to Hexham

*Start (700634)   Finish (940646)   Grade 1 – 2   Distance 19mls/30km (Haltwhistle (700634) to
Bardon Mill 6mls/10km   Bardon Mill to Haydon Bridge 5mls/8km   Haydon Bridge to
Warden Bridge 5½mls/9km   Warden Bridge to Hexham 2½mls/4km)*

From Haltwhistle the river is Grade 1 – 2. There is a large weir beneath Haltwhistle Viaduct (710637) which should be portaged on the right bank under the bridge. The rapids tend to be shallow in low water or bouncy in medium to high levels.

The River Allen flows in from the right three miles above Haydon Bridge. At Haydon Bridge there is a weir under the old bridge (843643) which should be taken through the far left-hand arch. In high levels it is advisable to inspect this weir beforehand. There is parking and access below the new bridge on the right-hand side (845644). The stretch from Haydon Bridge to Hexham is one of the most popular touring sections of the Tyne. It is generally Grade 1 – 2 with plenty of interest at this standard and is an attractive and enjoyable run.

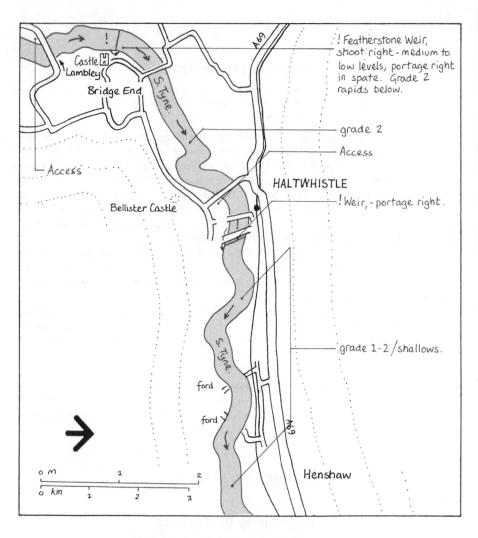

Take-outs on this section can be at Warden Bridge (910660) or at the confluence with the North Tyne (918660). The last section down to the Tyne Green at Hexham is deep and flat, providing a good area for training and teaching.

RIVER TYNE (SOUTH TYNE/RIVER ALLEN): STAGE 2A

Allenbridge to Plankey Mill

Start (800592) Finish (796622) Grade 2 – 3 Distance 3mls/5km
(Plankey Mill to Tyne 2mls/3km Grade 2 – 3)

The River Allen flows into the South Tyne three miles upstream of Haydon Bridge. Although relatively short in length, the section of the river between the confluence of the East and West Allen and the Tyne provides a committing descent of untamed wildwater. The deep and steeply forested valley sides of the Allen and the occasional inaccessible gorge give this river a feel of wilderness. With a scattering of large boulders and long continuous rapids it closely resembles an Alpine river, a quality which is enhanced when the level is high. It is best paddled in medium to high flows as anything lower makes some sections too low to navigate enjoyably.

The usual starting point is from the road bridge (800592) below the confluence of the East and West Allen rivers. Both these major tributaries can be paddled from higher up in high water conditions, although care is needed as fallen trees can often block the narrow channels. The run on the Allen is generally Grade 3, however in higher flows the

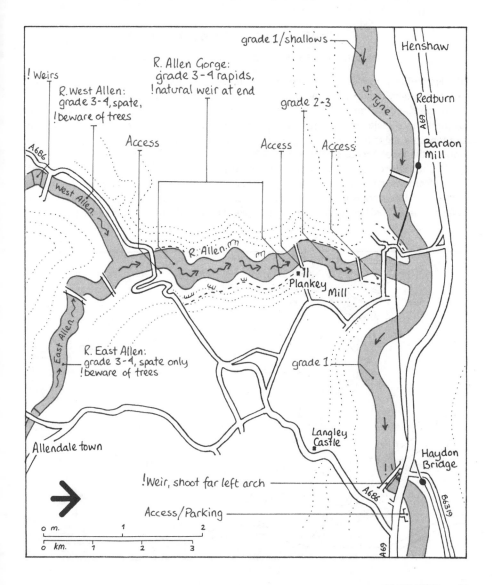

speed and continuity of the rapids and the occasional large stopper, especially on the large natural weir at the end, can increase the grading. Again, fallen trees can present a dangerous hazard and inspection of rapids when necessary is straightforward. On the natural weir the stopper is at its most powerful on the left, but can be run on the extreme left. Right of centre is generally the easiest route. The run can finish below the suspended footbridge at Plankey Mill or continue for another mile to the confluence with the Tyne and a run on down to Haydon Bridge.

RIVER TYNE (NORTH TYNE): STAGE 2B

Chollerford to South Tyne

Start (919704)   Finish (918660)   Grade 3   Distance 4mls/6km

The North Tyne from Chollerford to the confluence with the South Tyne offers a section of good quality Grade 2 – 3 paddling with one section of Grade 3 – 4. Releases of water from the Kielder Dam can improve the canoeing on this river so that the river has become a 'classic' stretch for whitewater training and wildwater racing. Access agreements exist for the lower part of the North Tyne and intending users should contact the local Access Officer for details.

At Chollerford put in above or below the weir, a long stopper forms on this in high water from which it can be difficult to escape. Just downstream on the right are the remains of Chesters Roman Fort. It was here that the Romans built a bridge across the river as part of Hadrian's Wall. There are several rapids of Grade 2 with occasional good

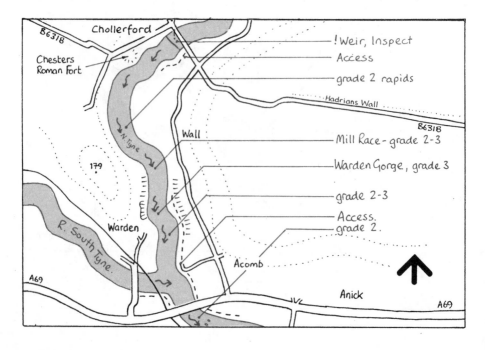

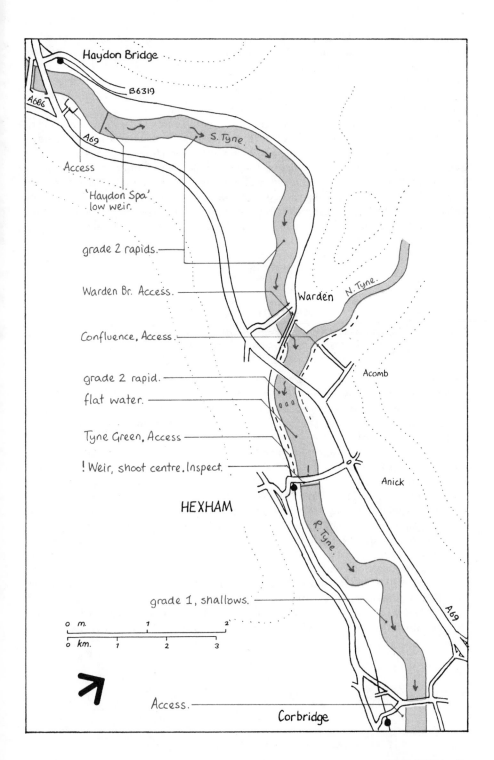

Haydon Bridge

B6319

A686

A69

S. Tyne

Access

'Haydon Spa'.
low weir.

grade 2 rapids.

Warden Br. Access.

Warden

N. Tyne.

Confluence, Access.

Acomb

grade 2 rapid.

flat water.

Tyne Green, Access

! Weir, shoot centre. Inspect.

HEXHAM

Anick

R. Tyne.

grade 1, shallows.

0   m.   1   2

0   km.   1   2   3

Access.

Corbridge

A69

A1

playspots in the right conditions; between them the river can be sluggish at times. A long rapid by the mill buildings on the left curves to the right, finishing in heavy standing waves and a large left-hand eddy. Downstream lies Warden Gorge. On either side there are steep banks and the rocky outcrop ahead on the right heralds the start. The first rapid can be run right or left; in the centre the river drops over a rock sill onto confused boulders which can produce a nasty stopper in high water.

A little further on lies the main section, one hundred yards of rapids which are very rocky in low water, but bouncy in medium to high water with some powerful stoppers to avoid. Large standing waves can form at the bottom in high flows and in high spate an awesome stopper can be found across the river. Below is a further section of rapids before the take-out at the confluence with the South Tyne. The gorge can easily be inspected beforehand by walking up the pathways from the confluence. For those of you who require liquid refreshment after a good morning's paddling, make for The Rat at Anick with its curious collection of bits and pieces on the walls and ceilings.

RIVER TYNE: STAGE 3

Hexham to Wylam

Start (940646)   Finish (119646)   Grade 1 – 2   Distance 13mls/20km
(Hexham to Corbridge 4mls/6km   Corbridge to Bywell 4mls/6km
Bywell to Wylam 5mls/8km   Wylam to Tynemouth (tidal) 20mls/32km)

Hexham Weir, immediately below the bridge, can be shot in the central area at all levels; however, it is wise to check the exact route beforehand from the bridge. During the close fishing season the weir should not be used for whitewater practice or playing except in spate conditions as the pool is an important resting place for salmon which can often be seen jumping the weir.

From Hexham to Corbridge it is Grade 1 with some fast choppy water and occasional shallows passable at all levels. Access at Corbridge is on the right below the bridge (989641) and from now on the river is mostly flat but there are some good Grade 1 – 2 rapids which are of interest. Riding Mill Weir (028621) should be inspected, especially at higher flows when a portage may be necessary. In low water it can be run on the right, however, safety cover is advisable due to the boxed-in stopper. This stretch of river is a good run when water levels are too low for the upper reaches of the Tyne catchment. At Wylam the river becomes tidal. Shoot left on Wylam Weir but beware of hidden stakes below the surface of the water.

Beyond Wylam and Newburn the river banks become industrialised and lined with wharfs and quaysides. This section holds its own interest as it flows into the heart of Newcastle and beneath the numerous bridges that span the Tyne. You can finish at the quayside on the left beyond the Tyne Bridge or continue on to Tynemouth and the North Sea.

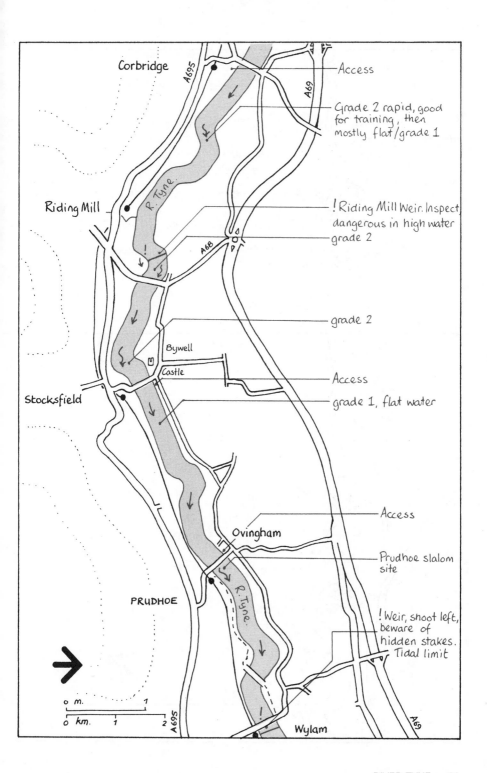

Corbridge ———— Access

Grade 2 rapid, good
for training, then
mostly flat/grade 1

R. Tyne

Riding Mill ———— ! Riding Mill Weir. Inspect,
dangerous in high water
grade 2

A68

grade 2

Bywell

Castle ———— Access

Stocksfield ———— grade 1, flat water

———— Access

Ovingham

———— Prudhoe slalom
site

PRUDHOE

R. Tyne

! Weir, shoot left,
beware of
hidden stakes.
Tidal limit

o m.   1
o km.   1   2

Wylam

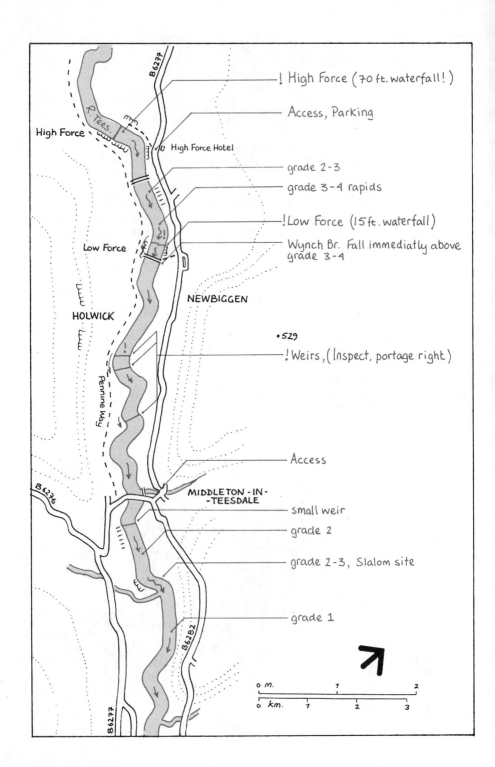

! High Force (70 ft. waterfall!)

Access, Parking

High Force Hotel

grade 2-3

grade 3-4 rapids

! Low Force (15 ft. waterfall)

Wynch Br. Fall immediatly above
grade 3-4

NEWBIGGEN

• 529

! Weirs, (Inspect, portage right)

Access

MIDDLETON - IN -
-TEESDALE

small weir

grade 2

grade 2-3, Slalom site

grade 1

High Force

R. Tees

Low Force

HOLWICK

Pennine Way

B 6277

B 6276

B 6282

B 6277

0 m.   1   2

0 km.   1   2   3

RIVER TEES

HIGH FORCE TO WINSTON

OS Sheet 92   23 miles/37km   Grade 3 – 4

Dominating the Northern Pennines the River Tees has carved a tortuous path through a multitude of geological features creating an ever-changing riverscape second to none. Hard igneous rock called Whin Sill over softer limestone has formed spectacular waterfalls and cascades, the High Force and Cauldron Snout being, respectively, the largest fall and cascade in England. Five reservoirs control the input into the river which is used as an open system to supply the needs of industrial Teeside some seventy miles down river.

Teesdale is known as the 'Forgotten Dale', having virtually only agriculture as its economic base. Tourism is now being encouraged as a viable alternative, for the valley is a land steeped in history and renowned for its spectacular river and landscape.

Amongst such sporting activities as skiing, sailing, riding, climbing, walking, fishing, etc., canoeing has long featured as part of the scene, just managing to live in relative harmony with the river's other uses.

For the canoeist the river provides some of England's finest wild water in a rugged outdoor environment, suitable for the intermediate to expert paddler, having little to offer the novice except capsizes, bone-crunching swims and lost boats.

The classic rapids are Low Force (Grade 3 – 4), Woden Croft (Grade 3 – 4) and Abbey Rapids (Grade 3 – 4), all of which can be raised up to Grade 5 – 6 in the river's infamous flash floods. The difficulty and seriousness of the river is increased by its course through a number of gorges where rescue and recovery are both difficult and hazardous. Each year there is an average of three or four fatalities – though the victims are not usually canoeists, for whom there is just a steady toll of wrecked canoes and broken bones. These challenging water conditions are found in the winter months with the summer usually offering low conditions which are generally unsuitable for even plastic boats.

Access considerations on the River Tees
Access is variable and may deteriorate because of problems on the other rivers and the growth of fishing interests. Contact the Local Access Officer or call in at 'Four Seasons' adventure store, 44 The Bank, Barnard Castle, for advice on river levels, problem areas and local canoeing events. This is particularly important during the fishing season between March and November.

High Force to Egglestone

*Start (881284)   Finish (996233)   Grade 3 – 4 High Force to Low Force   2 – 3 Low Force to Eggleston
Distance 9½mls/15km*

The start below the seventy-foot waterfall of High Force, hemmed in by vertical rock faces, is perhaps the most spectacular opening to any river trip in this country. It is tempting to paddle as close as possible to the fall but the force of the spray and the downdraught of wind make this virtually impossible, which is perhaps just as well. There is a path that leads from the High Force Hotel (885286) to the falls (an entrance fee is usually charged in the spring and summer months). It is well worth walking up to the top of the falls for the view downstream and to assure yourself that these falls really are uncanoeable.

This section of the river is best paddled in medium to high levels, as a good depth of water is often required to cover the many shallow and rocky features of the river bed.

The short run down from High Force to Low Force contains most of the difficult rapids. In high water it can increase by a full grade. Low Force is another waterfall with a tricky lead-in rapid, the first drop being only three to four feet, but with a second drop of fifteen feet. Inspection is essential and a throwline should be to hand if anyone is going to attempt the falls. Beware of the right-hand shoots on both drops as they can have very strong towbacks. It is best to choose a route with the least water going over it. In high levels Low Force is a thundering river-wide fall and not an inviting prospect.

Fifty yards beyond Low Force there is another small fall; again beware of the stopper in medium to high levels. A short distance below is Wynch Bridge which spans this small rocky gorge.

After Wynch Bridge the river is less technical but can produce a fast run in high water. There are three large weirs below Holwick, all about eight to ten feet in height. These should be inspected as there can be severe stoppers in medium to high water levels (portage on the right if necessary). The more interesting part of this section is from just before Middleton and just after. Below Middleton Bridge there is a small but easy weir followed by short rocky rapids to Leekworth Farm. This is a popular slalom venue with its Grade 2 – 3 rapids and tricky stoppers on the 'S' bend in high levels. After Leekworth the river widens with rocky gravel beds in low conditions to Eggleston Bridge.

Eggleston to Barnard Castle

Start (996233)   Finish (046167)   Grade 3 (4 in high water)   Distance 6mls/10km

The section from Eggleston Bridge to Cotherstone is known as the 'Racecourse' as it hosts a number of whitewater racing competitions each year. (*Note:* There are difficult access problems here – please refer to the river adviser before launching.) It is one of the best wild water stretches on the river, with up to three miles of Grade 3 rapids which can be Grade 4 in high water conditions. Much of this section is between gorges and high banks with dense woodland on either side. At Woden Croft there are long rapids on a series of bends with danger points coming into view at short notice. In the centre section the river impinges onto a large boulder with a tight route on the right and an easier route on the left. After 150 yards a small fall/chute is best shot left as there is a vicious stopper on the right in high water. In spate conditions the standards can be up to Grade 5 with large, unforgiving stoppers and a river-width stopper forming half a mile above Woden. This secluded area of the river is a haven for wildlife and it is preferable to canoe in smaller groups to lessen any environmental impact.

After Cotherstone the river presents few problems and is generally Grade 2. There is one Grade 3 fall which is best run on the right and is worth inspecting in high water for

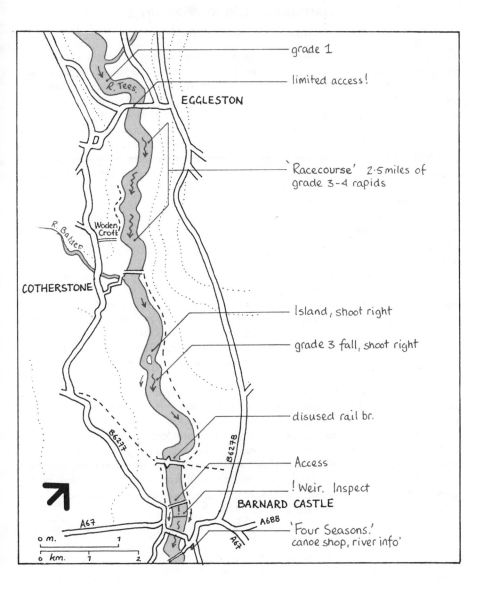

grade 1

limited access!

EGGLESTON

'Racecourse' 2·5 miles of grade 3-4 rapids

Island, shoot right

grade 3 fall, shoot right

disused rail br.

Access

! Weir. Inspect

BARNARD CASTLE

'Four Seasons.' canoe shop, river info'

the stoppers at the bottom (if necessary portage on the right). A good finishing point is at the footbridge just before Barnard Castle as beyond this is Barnard Castle Weir. This is dangerous and you must avoid the centre chute! There is a fish ladder on the left which should be inspected, although portage on the right is generally recommended. A short Grade 2 – 3 section leads on from the river to the road bridge.

Barnard Castle to Winston

Distance 7½mls/12km   Grade 3 – 4

After Barnard Castle the scenery becomes more varied, with gorge sections giving way to woodland and open farmland. This area is heavily fished, especially in spring and summer, but the water levels then are not usually suitable for canoeing. Access at the start is on the right bank near the footbridge south of the town. Immediately below is a small broken weir easily run down the centre. A few hundred yards down are the Mill Falls, a ledge drop with mill buildings on the left. This is best shot towards the right but it is preferable to inspect if you are at all uncertain of the best route. Abbey Rapids follow after half a mile and this is another popular slalom venue on the river. Here a long rapid (Grade 3 – 4) culminates in a narrow fall which is best run to the left as there can be vicious stoppers on the right.

Abbey Bridge is just downstream and beyond this the river enters a half-mile gorge with vertical walls up to thirty feet high. Rescue here is difficult, especially in medium to high levels when the water rushes through at a surprising speed, and a capsize at Abbey Rapids in these conditions could mean a long swim! Even in low to medium levels there are some tricky falls and rapids.

After the gorge there are a number of small rapids which represent no great problem until Whorlton Falls. The confluence of the Greta is passed on the right. This can be a good Grade 4 – 6 run but this is only possible in high water conditions.

Whorlton Falls is a long diagonal drop across the river with a strong towback. In low to medium conditions it is best run close to the main buttress on the right or to the far left at the end of the fall. Inspection is advised and portage is recommended on the right if you are in any doubt, or if the river is high, as a rescue from the mid-section would be very difficult.

After Whorlton there are a number of cataracts over Whin Sills to shoot. These long sloping rock ledges vary in severity according to water level. In medium to high levels beware of long stoppers across the river or parts of the river.

When Winston Bridge comes into view there are further rock ledges ahead to navigate. These can be Grade 2 – 3 depending on water levels but care must be taken in medium to high levels as there can be small but severe stoppers forming at certain places. A final easy run takes you down to the bridge. Access is on the right above the bridge or on the left immediately below the bridge. Below Winston the river widens with rock and gravel banks and is generally Grade 1 – 2.

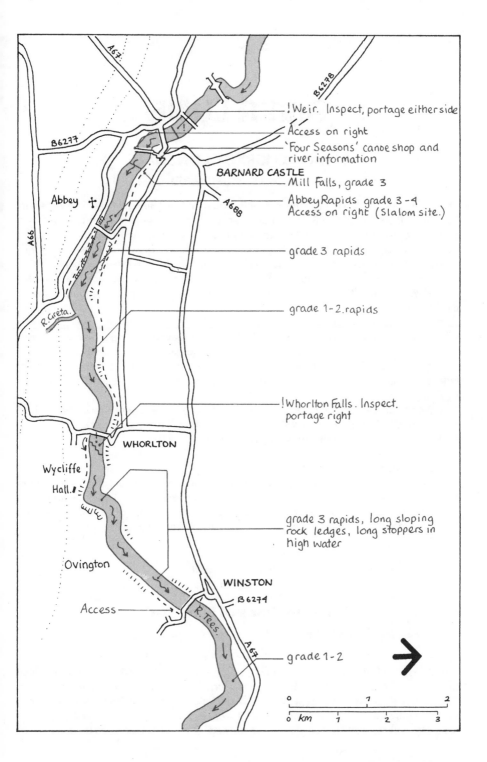

!Weir. Inspect, portage either side

Access on right

'Four Seasons' canoe shop and river information

BARNARD CASTLE

Mill Falls, grade 3

Abbey Rapids grade 3-4
Access on right (Slalom site.)

grade 3 rapids

grade 1-2 rapids

!Whorlton Falls. Inspect. portage right

WHORLTON

grade 3 rapids, long sloping rock ledges, long stoppers in high water

WINSTON

B6274

grade 1-2

Abbey

A66

R. Greta.

Wycliffe

Hall.

Ovington

Access

R. Tees.

A67

B6277

A67

B6278

A688

0   1   2
0   km   1   2   3

RIVER LUNE

TEBAY TO KIRKBY LONSDALE

OS Sheets 91/97/98   20miles/32km   Grade 2 – 3 (some 3 – 4)

The River Lune rises in the Northern Pennines just north of Howgill Fells. The waters of Sandwath Beck, Weasdale Beck and Bowderdale Beck combine to form the river as it crosses flat moorland in a westerly direction towards Tebay. At Tebay the river turns southwards, snaking under the M6 motorway and adjacent railway before rushing into a small gorge. Below, the river is bounded by steep hillsides and tree-lined banks with a consistent pace of small rapids. The occasional narrow chute and technical boulder choke, combined with small rocky gorges, add extra excitement to a superbly scenic canoeing river.

As the hills flatten out just south of Sedbergh there are two weirs which require caution and may need portage. Below, the River Rawthey, another popular whitewater river, joins the Lune, adding to its volume as it flows toward Kirkby Lonsdale. The river is now calmer with the odd small shingly rapid until the approach to Kirkby Lonsdale, where once again its pace increases as it flows down to the historic Devil's Bridge just beyond the town.

Beyond Kirkby Lonsdale the river continues for another twenty miles or so, less hurried than before except for a weir and rapid at Halton. Finally it passes Lancaster and flows into a tidal estuary that opens out into Morecambe Bay.

Access considerations on the River Lune

Access to the Lune is generally good during the salmon close season. Permission is required for the lower Lune, Rigmaden to Kirkby Lonsdale. At Beck Foot (Crook of Lune Bridge) cars should be parked at the viaduct and minibuses should avoid the narrow lanes. Full details of access are obtainable from the Local Access Officer (BCU).

RIVER LUNE: STAGE 1

Tebay to Crook of Lune Bridge

Start (619055)   Finish (620963)   Grade 2 – 3 (Fall at Tebay Gorge, 4)   Distance 6mls/10km

Taking Junction 38 off the M6 will bring you into Tebay. The left-hand exit on the roundabout will take you past the service station and along the B6260, to cross the river just north of old Tebay (619055). From this bridge you can see the river stretching eastward across a wide valley with the Howgill Fells on the right. To the west the river heads towards the first of four bridges as it weaves its way beneath the M6. There are several small rapids (Grade 1 – 2), some formed by old weir blocks, as the river flows

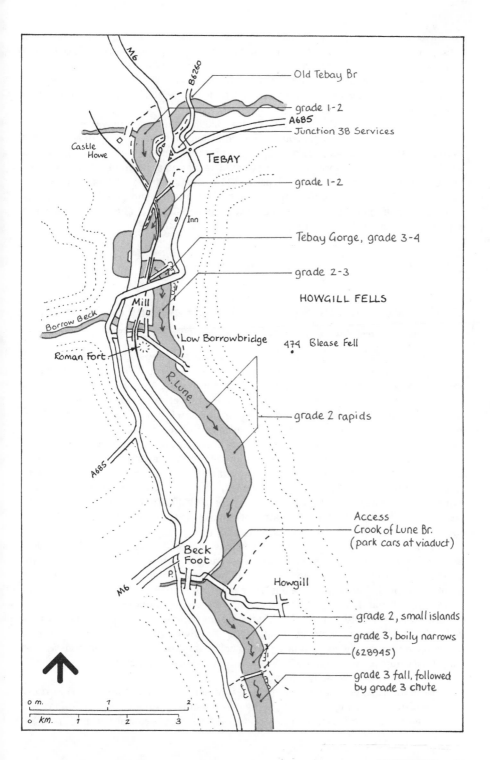

Old Tebay Br

grade 1-2

A685

Junction 38 Services

TEBAY

grade 1-2

Tebay Gorge, grade 3-4

grade 2-3

HOWGILL FELLS

Castle Howe

Inn

Mill

Borrow Beck

Roman Fort

Low Borrowbridge

474 Blease Fell

R. Lune

grade 2 rapids

A685

Access
Crook of Lune Br.
(park cars at viaduct)

Beck Foot

M6

P.

Howgill

grade 2, small islands

grade 3, boily narrows

(628945)

grade 3 fall, followed
by grade 3 chute

o m.   1   2

o km.   1   2   3

southwards to Tebay Gorge (613028). The river passes under the M6 for the final time, and then the railway line, before turning sharply into a rocky narrow gorge below an old road bridge. There is a Grade 4 rapid here as the river constricts between vertical rock walls. The rapid can be easily surveyed in advance from the bridge. Another series of rapids (Grade 3) follow on as the river passes beneath the A685 road bridge before the gorge opens out.

From Tebay Gorge to Crook of Lune Bridge (620963), there are many small Grade 2 – 3 rapids which can be fast and bouncy in high water. On either side there are wooded banks and steep hillsides providing a quiet and scenic run. If you want to avoid the difficult rapid at Tebay Gorge the journey could be started at Borrowbridge – a narrow stone structure which crosses the river at 612009. Just upstream of this bridge where Borrow Beck flows into the river there is an old mill and the site of a Roman fort. It is three and a half miles between Low Borrowbridge and Crook of Lune where the exit is on the right, just beyond the bridge by a small tributary stream.

RIVER LUNE: STAGE 2

Crook of Lune Bridge to the River Rawthey confluence

Start (620963)   Finish (629897)   Grade 3   Distance 5mls/8km

Crook of Lune Bridge is a favourite starting point for many canoeists. It is reached from a turning off the B6257 (616965) which descends under the viaduct down a narrow road to the river. After unloading, cars should be left at the viaduct. An island just downstream from the bridge acts as a good indicator to the river level – at low levels it is a shallow scrape down the right-hand side and at medium levels it is a gentle but fast rapid. From here there are small Grade 2 rapids with excellent spots for practising break-in and break-out techniques, and several fast bouncy channels around small islands.

A mile south of Crook of Lune the river constricts into a narrow channel, hemmed in by bedrock on the right and a rocky cliff on the left. It is a fast and long rapid with unpredictable swirly boils but it is an easy straight run down with large break-outs at the bottom. Below this a footbridge crosses the river (628945). There is a footpath up to the B6257 on the right or, on the left, a path that connects to the Dales Way, a long-distance footpath that parallels the Lune for part of its course.

Below the footbridge is a small fall with a diagonal stopper on the left but a straightforward shoot on the right that gives rise to a narrow standing wave ideal for playing and surfing. Another rock channel follows on, this one being more tricky (Grade 3), but only for its drop in gradient and boily water conditions. It is a straightforward run down through standing waves, stoppers and haystacks, to emerge in calm water.

The river now enters a small secluded gorge (Grade 2 – 3 rapids) that finishes beneath the disused railway viaduct (630931). The river opens out and is easier for a short while until the A684 road bridge – Lincoln's Inn Bridge – comes into view. Just before this there is a tricky Grade 3 – 4 rapid where the river is constricted between rocks and rushes into unstable boily water below.

Lincoln's Inn Bridge takes its name from a former hostelry, although only a farm now remains. From this bridge (632923) the river negotiates another couple of Grade 2 – 3 rapids before running into more rocky reefs. Here there are awkward drops (Grade 3 –

1 River Tees - at High Force

2 River Tees – Low Force in high water conditions

3 River Lune – below the Crook of Lune

4 River Tees – between High Force and Low Force

5   River Eden – the gorge below Lazonby

6   River Dart – below New Bridge

7 River Orchy – shooting the Grade 4 rapids below the Bridge of Orchy Hotel

8   River Findhorn – in the gorge.

9 (Above) River Spey – on the run down to Tamdhu Distillery

10 River Spey – the lower reaches seen from the Earth Pillars of Ordiequish

11 *River Orchy – above the Falls of Orchy*

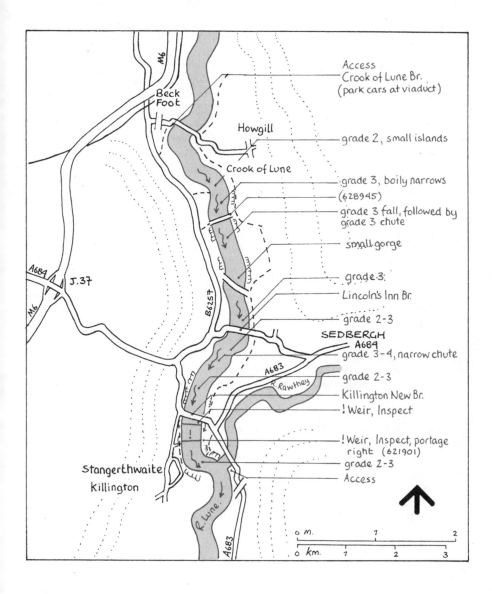

Access
Crook of Lune Br.
(park cars at viaduct)

grade 2, small islands

grade 3, boily narrows
(628945)

grade 3 fall, followed by
grade 3 chute

small gorge

grade 3:

Lincoln's Inn Br.

grade 2-3

SEDBERGH
A684
grade 3-4, narrow chute

grade 2-3

Killington New Br.

! Weir, Inspect

! Weir, Inspect, portage
right (621901)

grade 2-3

Access

4), the final one being where the river is forced into a very narrow chute with an awkward stopper and cross currents. It is easy to inspect these rapids, and to portage if desired, on the right. Another scenic gorge encloses the river with small Grade 2 – 3 rapids and rocky cliffs on either side before Killington New Bridge is reached (623908). The trip can finish here for convenient access to the road and to avoid the two weirs between here and the Rawthay confluence.

Below Killington New Bridge the first weir is a small drop across the river which, when levels are low, is best taken at speed on the left. But if levels are high there can be a large and dangerous towback and it should be portaged. If you are unsure about the level then it is essential to inspect this weir beforehand. It is then an easy run down to the next weir.

The second weir – Stangerthwaite Weir (621901) – is dangerous and caution should be exercised on approach. It has a large drop with a severe stopper and debris below. In low water it can be run over the step on the left but if you have any doubt in your ability to negotiate the correct line then portage the weir on the right. Below the weir, natural and man-made obstructions create a Grade 3 rapid as the river flows into a final small gorge before opening out to the confluence with the River Rawthey, with an exit on the left just beyond the junction.

RIVER LUNE: STAGE 3

River Rawthey confluence to Kirkby Lonsdale

Start (620963)   Finish (629897)   Grade 1 – 2   Distance 9mls/15km

Below the confluence with the Rawthey the Lune calms down into a pleasant scenic run. Periodically there are small shingly rapids and the wooded banks part occasionally to reveal views of green and rounded hills. Rigmaden Bridge (617849) is reached after three miles and beyond that the river twists in large meanders around Holme House. On one rapid a solitary tree stands alone on a shingle bank in the river, seemingly defiant against many years of spate conditions.

Barbon Beck enters the Lune on the left and soon afterwards a stone-turreted bridge comes into view, with steep and precipitous cliffs of red conglomerate on the right. A long Grade 2 rapid runs down to a right-hand bend. This has steep banks on either side forming a deep gorge with occasional Grade 2 rapids that can be more difficult depending on the river level. The river emerges from this wooded gorge into a long straight down to Kirkby Lonsdale and the local beauty spot of Ruskin's View. A bouncy right-hand channel around a long island brings you to the last few hundred yards before the historic stone arches of the Devil's Bridge are reached. It is a long run from the Rawthey confluence to the Devil's Bridge but the gentle scenic pace of the river and the final deep and wooded gorges makes it all worthwhile. Exit right just above the bridge and portage to the car-park at the eastern end of the bridge.

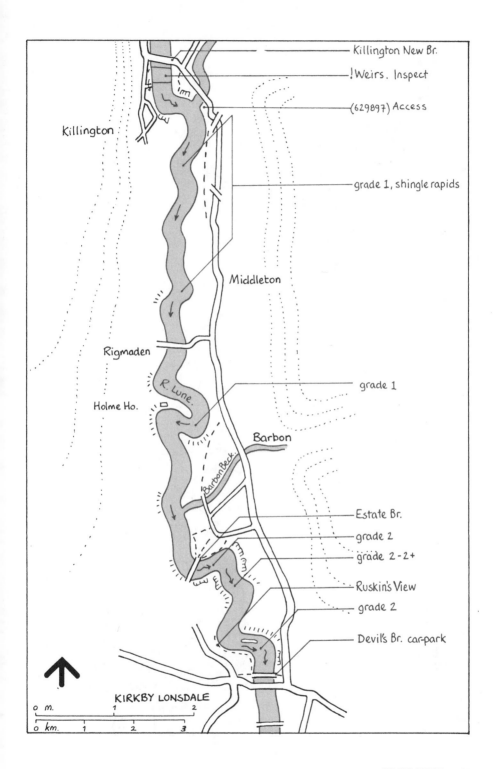

Killington New Br.

!Weirs. Inspect

(629897) Access

Killington

grade 1, shingle rapids

Middleton

Rigmaden

grade 1

R. Lune.

Holme Ho.

Barbon

Barbon Beck.

Estate Br.

grade 2

grade 2-2+

Ruskin's View

grade 2

Devil's Br. car-park

KIRKBY LONSDALE

0 m.   1   2

0 km.   1   2   3

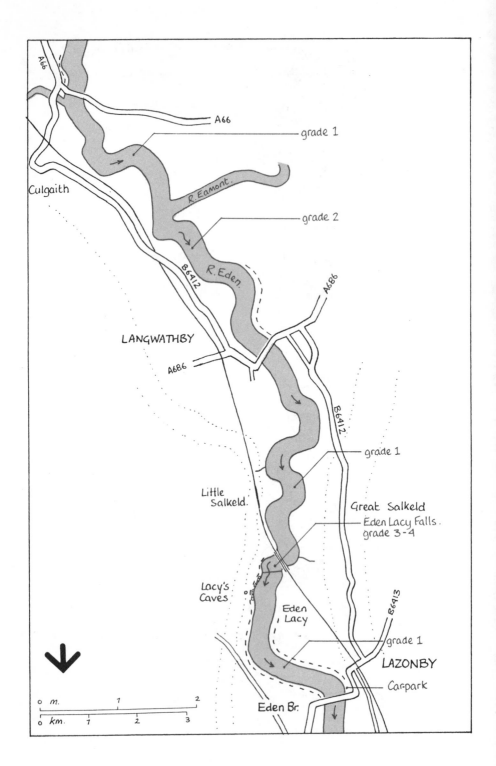

RIVER EDEN

CULGAITH TO WETHERAL

OS Sheets 85/86/90/91   25 miles/40km   Grade 1 – 2 (some 3)

The River Eden rises in the northern end of the Yorkshire Dales National Park from the same watershed that gives rise to the River Ure, which runs off to the east through Wensleydale. From its humble beginnings it drops swiftly through the deep valley of Mallerstang Common, fed by streams that run off the adjacent fells. From Kirkby Stephen the river begins its meandering journey bounded by undulating countryside to the west and the Pennines to the east. For much of its length the river is wide and calm, with the occasional small rapid, ideal for canoe touring. However, beyond Lazonby the character of the river changes considerably as it enters steep wooded valleys frequently flanked by precipitous rocky cliffs and periodically offering entertaining small rapids – an attractive proposition for canoeists seeking solitude and wilderness. This section of river, from Lazonby to Wetheral, is one of outstanding natural beauty suitable for both canoes and kayaks, with rapids that at the most reach Grade 3 but are generally no more than Grade 2. Beyond Wetheral and Warwick Bridge the land becomes flat and uninteresting as the River Eden flows on towards Carlisle. The valley is well worth inspection even if you are without a canoe as there are attractive footpaths along its banks giving quiet and scenic walks.

Access considerations on the River Eden
A comprehensive access agreement exists for the Eden between Lazonby and Armathwaite Weir. For details of this agreement and the access above and below contact the Local River Adviser (BCU).

RIVER EDEN: STAGE 1

Upper Eden A66 Bridge to Lazonby, Eden Bridge

Start (604281)   Finish (551404)   Grade 1 – 2 (3 – 4 weir)   Distance 11½mls/18km

The Upper Eden, from Appleby in Westmorland down to where the A66 crosses the river (604281), is gentle and meandering, passing open fields and the occasional steep wooded bank. It continues in the same vein from the A66 bridge to the confluence with the River Eamont (587310) which flows out of Ullswater and is itself a twelve-mile, Grade 1 – 2 run. Soon after the confluence there are Grade 2 rapids but then the river calms down again and reaches Langwathby Bridge (566335) after five miles.

From Langwathby it is six miles to Eden Bridge and the river begins to give a hint of the scenery that is to follow on the lower sections. After several large meanders the river takes a right-hand bend passing under the arches of the railway viaduct. Just after this is a natural weir, Eden Lacy Falls (563379), Grade 3 – 4. It can be run on the far right, or far left, but in higher flows must be inspected as a large stopper forms along its length. On the right are steep wooded slopes and sandstone cliffs with, a little further down on the right, the curious arched windows and chambers of Lacy's Caves (564383). From here it is two miles of easy going to Eden Bridge at Lazonby.

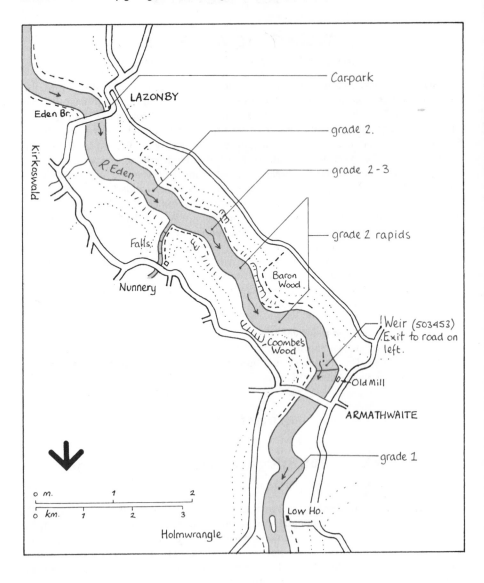

Eden Bridge to Armathwaite Weir

Start (551404)   Finish (503453)   Grade 2 (some 3)   Distance 5mls/8km

This section of the Eden has become a popular venue not only for recreational canoeists but also for river racing competitions. It is a suitable section for canoeists of all levels of ability with many Grade 2 rapids that can rise to Grade 3 in certain conditions. The river flows through a wide, steep-sided, forested gorge with tall sandstone outcrops and cliffs giving an air of seclusion and remoteness from the outside world. There is a car-park at Eden Bridge which provides a convenient place to start.

From Eden Bridge a longish section of flat water is travelled before the first of many Grade 2 rapids is reached. Just below Nunnery a tributary stream, Croglin Water, enters the Eden and, if you have time, pull in here and take a walk up its side to view the narrow chasms through which this stream flows and cascades. Below the confluence there is a path cut into the sandstone cliff on the right. On the left a towering outcrop of rock marks the beginning of a long Grade 2 – 3 rapid, rocky in low water but fast and exciting in high water. There are plenty of smaller rapids that follow this, with many playspots. A long cliff is reached on the left and further on down, on the right, another rocky outcrop below Coombe's Wood on which you may see the occasional climber scrambling around.

As you pass this cliff keep an eye out for the sad and smiling faces carved into the sandstone on the right, and an inscription that reads 'Oh the fisher's gentle life, happiest is of any, void of pleasure, full of strife and beloved by many. Other joys are but toys and to be lamented, only this a pleasure is . . . fishing'. Its author obviously had not tried canoeing!

Although the rapids have now subsided the scenic surroundings maintain the interest and character of the river to Armathwaite Weir (503453). This is a natural rock sill that has been used as a convenient weir for an old mill further down on the left. In low water the river runs only on the right (Grade 3 – 4) and will require inspection. In high levels this weir can be very dangerous so you may wish to finish your journey here and exit on the left by a stone shed and walk up to the road. This is a convenient egress point as only a long flat section remains to Armathwaite Bridge (507460).

Armathwaite Bridge to Wetheral

Start (507460)   Finish (469543)   Grade 1 – 2   Distance 8½mls/14km

Below Armathwaite the river is smooth and calm, with fields on the left. At Holmwrangle the river diverges around an island with the occasional small rapid to speed you onwards. A mile and a half beyond the island the banks steepen once again into woodlands. There is a Grade 2 rapid where the river flows over a small drop in the bedrock. Fishgarth Wood is on the right and another island is reached with shallow rapids around the right-hand channel. This is a prime fishing area and the fishermen often use rowing boats to find the best spot, proving that unpowered craft and the

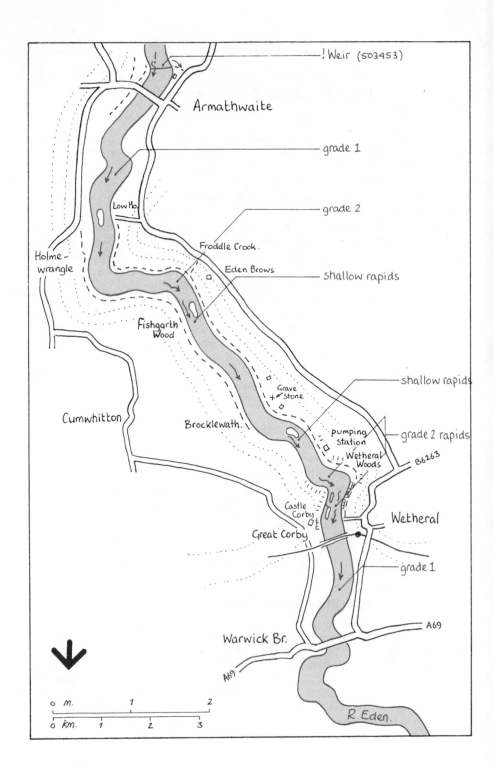

! Weir (503453)

Armathwaite

grade 1

grade 2

Low Ho

Froddle Crook.

Eden Brows

shallow rapids

Holme-
wrangle

Fishgarth
Wood

Grave
Stone

shallow rapids

Cumwhitton

Brocklewath.

pumping
Station

grade 2 rapids

Wetheral
Woods

B6263

Castle
Corby

Wetheral

Great Corby

grade 1

Warwick Br.

A69

A69

R.Eden.

m.   1   2

km.   1   2   3

splash of oars do little to disturb the fish below. Likewise you too should pass considerately along this quiet scenic stretch of river. Below Fishgarth Woods the banks open out into fields. Further on yet another island is encountered, again the right-hand channel takes the main flow over more shallow rapids. Below, on the left, is Wetheral pumping station. This heralds the start of the final section where the banks steepen once more as the river passes through Wetheral Woods. There is a steep rocky cliff ahead as the river turns sharp right into a long section of Grade 2 rapids over shallow rock beds. The main flow of the river runs to the left of a long island and it is best to keep to this side to avoid the constrictions and sluice on the right-hand channel.

Directly ahead and high above is Castle Corby. This large house is perched on the edge of precipitous red sandstone cliffs and just to the right are ornamental gardens with steps leading down to the river. The river then turns to the left for the final straight to Wetheral. It is only a hundred yards or so to where a road comes down to the river, which is a convenient finishing point. Beyond is the railway viaduct with shallow rapids below. Another mile and a half brings you to Warwick Bridge and another possible finishing point, for after this the river passes Holme Eden Abbey and the land becomes flat and uninteresting.

RIVER DART

DARTMEET TO DARTMOUTH

OS Sheets 191/202   30 miles/48km   Grade 3 – 4 (upper river)   1 – 2 (lower river)

The River Dart provides a good variety of paddling for canoeists of all abilities, the upper stretches giving some of the best and most popular whitewater canoeing in the South West, the central ones an interesting introduction for novice or low grade paddlers and the lower reaches ideal opportunity for touring in both kayaks and open Canadian canoes.

The Dart derives its name and its water from the granite uplands of Dartmoor and, with the large catchment area and narrow confines, it can change from a rocky stream into a raging torrent in a matter of hours, and vice versa. (*Note:* During and after a heavy rainfall the river can rise or fall by about 10cm every hour.) The upper stretches are best paddled after some rainfall so that most of the boulders are covered.

Below Holne Bridge the river provides scenic paddling at all water levels with the five weirs being the only obstacles, all of which can be portaged.

At Totnes the river becomes tidal and provides excellent touring opportunities, although the weir above Totnes and the Town Bridge at low tide provide some interest for novice whitewater paddlers.

Access to the river is good, with all points not too far from the A38, although car-parking space is limited at Holne Bridge, Buckfast and Staverton.

Access considerations on the River Dart
All non-tidal sections of the River Dart are covered by an access agreement with the landowners and fishermen. This defines the egress points and when the river may be paddled.

Full details of the agreement and permission to use the river should be sought from the Regional Access Officer in advance of any planned trip. The tidal reaches of the Dart are controlled by the Dartmouth Harbour Authority and, although open, a licence should be obtained.

RIVER DART: STAGE 1

Dartmeet to New Bridge

Start (672732)   Finish (711709)   Grade 3 – 4   Distance 5mls/8km

This very steep section provides almost continuous Grade 3 – 4 rapids at a reasonable water level (gauged from the rock ledges at New Bridge – see next section), becoming almost unnavigable in low water and in high water turning into an Alpine-style descent with numerous large stoppers. A paddle on this section should not be taken lightly – there is no vehicular access as the river runs down a steep-sided wooded valley. The closest points are Dartmeet (the start) and New Bridge (the finish) and a path leading to the mid-point of this section from Venford Reservoir after approx two miles.

At Dartmeet (convenient car-park) take care to launch at the *confluence* of the West and East Dart. Do not launch into the East Dart which is a spawning ground at this point. The fun begins almost immediately with almost continuous Grade 3 rapids for about a mile. Within half a mile Coombstone Island is reached and the left-hand channel, although narrow, carries a deeper flow of water. The rapids maintain their difficulty at Grade 3 – 4 on the run down to Lucky Tor where a small island is run down the main channel on the left.

The rock faces of Lucky Tor can be seen high up on the left bank. Immediately after another island, which is also run on the left, there is a tricky boulder field leading to the first major fall where the river is channelled into a six-foot wide gap. After the fall Venford Brook enters on the right. Here there is a path that follows the brook up to the road at Venford Reservoir.

After Venford Brook continuous Grade 3 – 4 rapids follow on what is now the steepest section of the river – in the five miles between Dartmeet and New Bridge the river loses 800ft in height.

Bell Pool Island marks the beginning of another series of drops. The main channel runs to the right of the island and a few small drops lead quickly on to 'Euthanasia Falls', mid-way down the island.

Here the river runs over a sloping rock shelf and drops into a diagonal stopper. The main flow of water piles onto a large rock which guards a narrow exit. Like all good rapids, if your line is correct at the top then it all falls into place but if you make an error then . . . there's a good tale to tell in the pub afterwards.

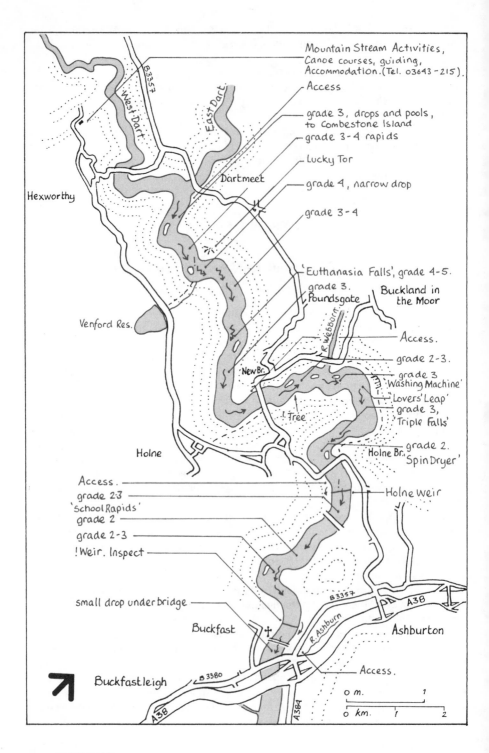

Mountain Stream Activities,
Canoe courses, guiding,
Accommodation. (Tel. 03643-215).

Access

grade 3, drops and pools,
to Combestone Island

grade 3-4 rapids

Lucky Tor

grade 4, narrow drop

grade 3-4

'Euthanasia Falls', grade 4-5.

grade 3.
Poundsgate

Buckland in
the Moor

Access.

grade 2-3.

grade 3
'Washing Machine'

'Lovers' Leap'
grade 3,
'Triple Falls'

grade 2.
'Spin Dryer'

Holne Br.

Holne Weir

Access.
grade 2-3
'School Rapids'
grade 2

grade 2-3

!Weir. Inspect

small drop under bridge

Buckfast

Ashburton

Access.

Buckfastleigh

0 m.   1

0 km.   1   2

West Dart

East Dart

Dartmeet

Hexworthy

Venford Res.

New Br.

! Tree

Holne

R. Webburn

R. Ashburn

B3357

B3357

A38

A38

A384

B3380

From Euthanasia Falls the river maintains consistency with many Grade 3 drops on a long straight run. There is one notable fall where it narrows down and drops six feet but this rarely presents problems. Rapids continue to New Bridge where you should exit at the steps on the left-hand bank immediately above the bridge to reach a convenient and *de rigeur* car-park.

RIVER DART: STAGE 2

New Bridge to Holne Bridge

Start (711709)   Finish (730706)   Grade 2 – 3   Distance 3mls/5km

This, the most popular section of the river, is known as 'The Loop'. It is an ideal training ground for intermediate paddlers and upwards as there are many rapids of varying difficulty. It is at its best in a medium to high water level, which can be gauged from the rock ledge at the bottom of the steps from New Bridge car-park.

When the water is below the ledge the river is low and many rocks will be exposed making boat-crunching almost unavoidable. The ideal level is when the water is up to the ledge, when most of the rocks will be covered and the rapids will be well-defined. When the river level is over the ledge and up to the steps then high water conditions are to be expected and overhanging trees become a major hazard.

The run begins with Grade 2 – 3 boulder rapids interspersed with deep pools. Nearly half a mile after New Bridge the main flow of the river runs to the right of a wooded island. Care should be taken on this stretch as there is at least one prominent tree (usually marked with orange tape) jutting out from the right-hand bank that should be avoided. Grade 2 – 3 rapids continue to the confluence with the River Wedburn, a tributary joining from the left.

A few hundred yards after the Webburn confluence is 'The Washing Machine', a Grade 3 rapid with a four-foot drop. In high water a large and vicious stopper forms on the right-hand side and consequently it is usually run to the left.

A long straight run leads into a right-hand bend, and this marks the beginning of 'Lovers' Leap' rapids, the longest stretch of whitewater on this section, where a hundred yards of boulder rapids lead towards the sheer rock wall of Lovers' Leap. This rocky outcrop comes into view half-way down the rapid. There is a small pool before the final rapid. The main flow runs into the rock wall which is undercut, and canoeists should keep well to the right.

Various Grade 2 rapids follow as the river continues down the deep wooded valley.

Half a mile beyond Lovers' Leap a left-hand channel takes the majority of the flow round a long island. The next major rapids are 'Triple Falls', three consecutive drops each between two and four feet high. The first is a single shoot on the left-hand side, ideal for pop-outs. The second is small and obvious but the third is slightly more tricky with a left-hand turn and a large rock or stopper (depending on the level) in the middle.

From Triple Falls a mainly flat section follows before 'The Spin Dryer', a large recirculating eddy on the final bend before Holne Bridge. This is visible from the layby on the road. At Holne Bridge exit on the right bank just beyond the bridge. Cars should be parked on the side of the road or in the layby, taking care not to obstruct access to the Country Park or local houses.

Holne Bridge to Buckfast

Start (730706) Finish (745668) Grade 2 plus two weirs Distance 3½ml/5km

This section is ideal for canoeists of all abilities, with the only major hazards being Holne and Furzeleigh weirs, both of which may be portaged. When combined with Section 2 this makes an excellent day's paddle.

Holne Weir is about 600 yards downstream of the bridge and consists of a vertical drop of three feet, with the main chute in the centre. In high water the central chute has a large towback, and the sill is undercut. Inspection is recommended from the right-hand bank bearing in mind the option to shoot on the left-hand side by an easier line.

Below the Holne Weir, in about 400 yards, there is the largest set of rapids of the section, 'School Rapids' (Grade 2), alongside the River Dart Country Park assault course. These are straightforward, apart from the large rock with a stopper towards the bottom.

The river continues with small drops and boulder fields until Buckfast Abbey comes into view, and you approach Furzeleigh Weir. Land on the left-hand side to inspect: it can be shot right of centre, or it can be run down the steps with care! Rescue is not easy in high water, and a long throw-line is required. Below Furzleigh Weir the river runs in a narrow channel, with a tricky drop where it passes under the footbridge, down to the road bridges by the A38. The best exit point is the confluence with the River Ashburn (on the left between the two road bridges). Drag the canoe up this small tributary, under the flood tunnel, and exit left across fields to the Ashburton road.

Buckfast to Staverton

Start (745668) Finish (785637) Grade 2 plus one weir Distance 4½mls/7km

This section is mainly on flat water flowing through a wooded valley with the occasional small rapid. The Dart Valley Steam Railway runs alongside the river from Buckfast to Totnes via Staverton and the A384 is close at hand.

From the Ashburton road (7456668) cross fields to the the River Ashburn which usually contains enough water to paddle the short distance down to the Dart (through a flood tunnel).

Salmon Ponds Weir, just below Buckfast, needs some care, especially in high water. The weir has seven steps, starting large and getting smaller. The first two also have a chute (just wide enough for a boat) which provides an easy route, and the others are only about four inches high and do not cause problems, provided they are taken straight.

The only other hazard is Hood Weir, below Riverford Bridge. This weir is breached, but the current leads close to tree roots on the right-hand side. Finish under the road bridge at Staverton, where there is a sandy beach on the left with access to the road.

Staverton to Totnes

Start (785637)   *Finish* (806596)   *Grade* 1 plus two weirs   *Distance* 4½mls/7km

This is a beautiful paddle through the Dart Valley, and around the grounds of Dartington Hall.

Staverton Weir, about 400 yards below the bridge, can be shot at the right-hand end, but beware of two concrete blocks at the bottom of the chute. The remainder of the weir is normally dry, except in high water when trees below the weir become a hazard. Once past the shallow rapids below the weir the river becomes placid and quiet.

The final weir at Totnes can be taken along the diagonal wall in low water, or straight down the centre if there is sufficient depth. Keep clear of the salmon steps on the left-

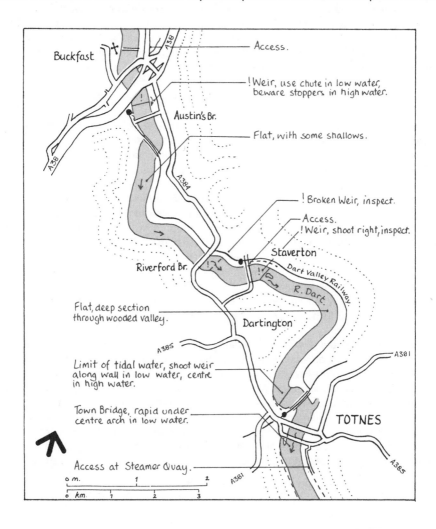

hand side (and fishermen). The river now becomes tidal and at low water forms small rapids under the railway bridge and Totnes town bridge. These rapids along with Totnes Weir can provide a useful training ground during the summer months, although access to the weir is restricted to three hours either side of high tide by arrangement with the angling club.

RIVER DART: STAGE 6

Totnes to Dartmouth (Kingswear)

Start (806596)   Finish (881512)   Grade Tidal   *Distance 10m/16km*

From the Steamer Quay at Totnes (easy parking, currently 40p a day) the river meanders gently between tree-lined banks, with several small creeks that are worth exploring, especially Bow Creek which is navigable at high tide up to Tuckenhay. At the start the river is twenty-five yards wide, increasing to almost a mile at its widest point. An abundance of wildlife can be spotted along the banks, particularly near the Heronry and during one trip we were actually accompanied by a seal, much to one lady's surprise when it popped up next to her canoe. The trees thin out at intervals providing good picnic sites, but beware of the thick mud at low tide. Traditional salmon fishing can often be observed in the upper part.

Two miles below Totnes, high above the river on the right, is Sharpham House, now owned by the National Trust, with the Heronry opposite. After another three miles there is the small harbour of Stoke Gabriel tucked away behind a headland on the left, with Bow Creek opposite. Stoke Gabriel is a small village that has found a novel solution to the problem of the unsightly expanses of mud at low tide. They have built a dam across the inlet to hold enough water to form a small lake, which proves a valuable tourist attraction. There are shops and a pub within a short walk of the waterfront.

The river now gets much wider, and can be rough in windy weather, so it is worth keeping close to the bank, and also keeping clear of the main channel, marked by red and green buoys, which is used by pleasure boats.

After seven miles Dittisham is reached. Here the river narrows again, and a small passenger ferry plies across to Greenham Quay. The current can become quite strong at this point, particularly during the ebb tide, when it can sweep you past the village before you have a chance to pull off should you wish to visit the pub or the shops on the waterfront.

Below Dittisham the river forms the harbour at Dartmouth, with numerous industrial sites along the bank, as well as the Royal Naval College Dockyard on the right. The Torbay and Dartmouth Steam Railway joins the river on the left and the town of Dartmouth comes into sight on the right, and the Upper Ferry, a chain-hauled car ferry from Dartmouth to Kingswear. Give it a wide berth, as the chains lie along the river bed and are lifted when the ferry crosses. There is access at several points along either bank (but NOT at the ferry slipways) but the easiest parking is on the Kingswear side (left bank) in a Pay-on-Exit car-park at the bottom of the hill. This can be reached from the river by paddling or walking under the small railway bridge just above the station.

For current information on river levels, access and details of canoe courses, contact Mountain Streams Activities, Hexworthy, Yelverton, Devon PL20 6SF (☎ 03643 215).

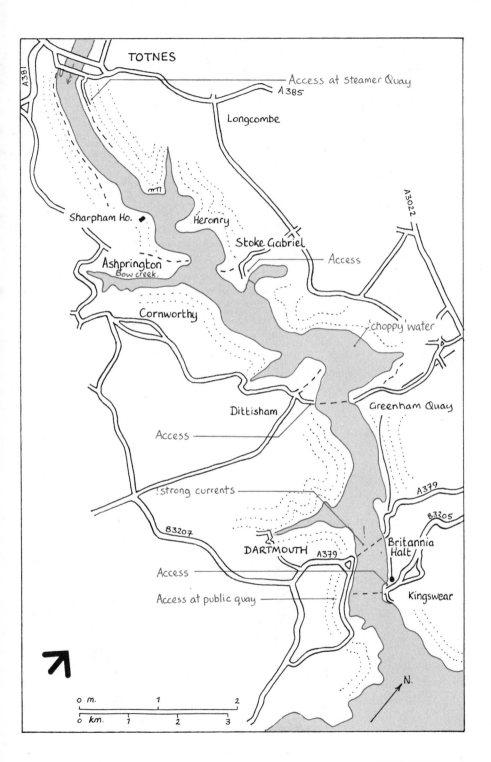

TOTNES

Access at steamer Quay

A385

Longcombe

A381

A3022

Sharpham Ho.

Heronry

Stoke Gabriel

Access

Ashprington

Bow creek.

Cornworthy

choppy water

Dittisham

Greenham Quay

Access

strong currents

A379

B3207

B3205

DARTMOUTH

A379

Britannia Halt

Access

Access at public quay

Kingswear

N.

o m.   1   2

o km.   1   2   3

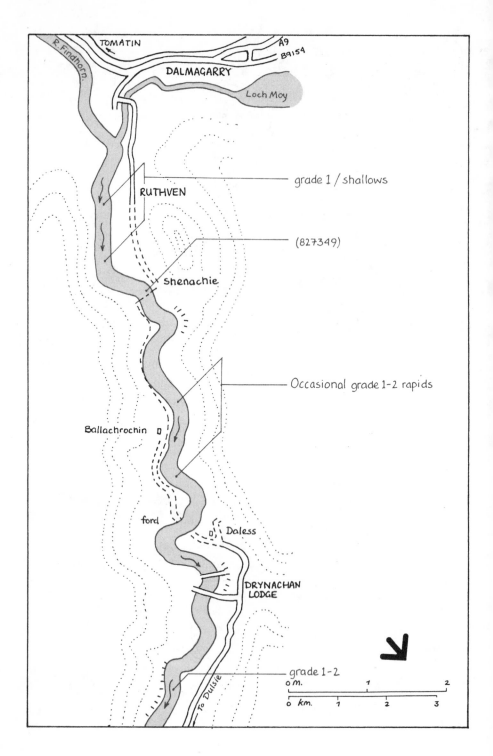

TOMATIN

R. Findhorn.

A9

B9154

DALMAGARRY

Loch Moy

grade 1 / shallows

RUTHVEN

(827349)

Shenachie

Occasional grade 1-2 rapids

Ballachrochin

ford

Daless

DRYNACHAN
LODGE

grade 1-2

To Dulsie

0 m.   1   2

0 km.   1   2   3

RIVER FINDHORN

RUTHVEN TO FORRES

OS Sheets 27/35   28½ miles/45km   Grade 3 – 4

"What spot on earth can exceed in beauty the landscape comprising the Old Bridge of Dulsie, spanning with its lofty arches the deep dark pool, shut in by grey and fantastic rocks, surmounted with the greenest of green swards with clumps of ancient weeping birches backed by dark pine trees."

This account of the River Findhorn at Dulsie Bridge written by Charles St John appeared in Murray's Handbook for Scotland 1894. Although a little romantic it is still an inspiring description, applicable to the river even today. With its scenic gorges and an excellent variety of canoeable sections of all gradings it ranks as one of the outstanding canoeing rivers in the British Isles.

The Findhorn rises in the Monadhliath Mountains and runs a course north-eastward across the barren moors of Moy and Dalarossie before turning northwards through a series of deep gorges to reach the sea at Findhorn Bay, where it flows into the Moray Firth. The Findhorn is an excellent fishing river with many small fishing huts along its banks and canoeists should keep an eye out for green-clad figures in the distance and exercise courtesy when passing.

For the whitewater paddler it is the lower reaches of the river that are the most interesting but for those who prefer something less life-threatening there are sections suitable for canoeists of all levels of competence and inclination, making it an ideal venue for mixed ability groups. The sections described may be combined to form longer sections if the prevailing conditions of weather, water level and enthusiasm are right.

Access considerations on the River Findhorn
Refer to the section 'Access in Scotland' on Page 9.

RIVER FINDHORN: STAGE 1

Ruthven to Drynachan Lodge

Start (815331)   Finish (865397)   Grade 1 – 2   Distance 6mls/10km

Continuing on the A9 north of Aviemore, the road crosses a high bridge over the River Findhorn. For those interested in exploring the upper reaches of the river, turn off at Tomatin to take the road that follows the river upstream. However, for the more interesting stretch that runs through a steep-sided and lonely moorland valley, carry on through Tomatin until you reach a road signposted to Ruthven. Take this turn-off (790320) to drop down to a small hump-backed bridge over Funtack Burn. The road runs parallel to the burn until it converges with the Findhorn. Here the river is wide with rapids over shingle banks. A canoe trip could start here where the road is conveniently close to the river, alternatively continue on to Ruthven (815331) and follow the road as it becomes a rough but driveable track to the small ruins of Shenachie (827349). There is a ropeway across the river here and a footpath that continues on the other side of the river. From here the river runs four miles down a remote valley with steep sides in a series of sweeping curves with the occasional Grade 1 – 2 rapid. The next habitation is Drynachan Lodge (865397), which is reached by road from Ruthven by a long, circuitous drive around the vast area of mountains and moors crossed by the river, via Carrbridge and Dulsie Bridge.

RIVER FINDHORN: STAGE 2

Drynachan Lodge to Dulsie Bridge

Start (865397)   Finish (932415)   Grade 1 – 3 (4)   Distance 5mls/8km

Drynachan Lodge (932415) is reached from Dulsie Bridge near the B9007 Carrbridge – Ferness road. You can drive beyond the Lodge to the farm at Daless where there is a ford in low water. This section is a prime fishing area and care should be taken not to disturb anglers. From Drynachan the river continues as Grade 1 – 2 until it reaches a footbridge beneath a rocky outcrop (913405). At this point a series of boulders constrict the flow forming Grade 2 – 3 rapids which can produce large stoppers in high flow conditions. The final half-mile to the Dulsie Gorge Bridge is calm. Those who are warmed up to the rapids may want to finish with a run of the gorge, a fast Grade 3 – 4, whilst others may want to exit just above on the right.

RIVER FINDHORN: STAGE 3

Dulsie Bridge to Ferness Bridge

Start (932415)   Finish (960462)   Grade 3 – 4   Distance 5½mls/9km

Dulsie Bridge spans the grey rock walls just below a small gorge. The name Dulsie is derived from 'Dulthasaid' meaning 'Meadow of the Stance' and the bridge was erected in 1764, forming an important link in the military road from Perth to Fort George by Grantown on Spey. The rapids of Dulsie Bridge can be viewed easily from a path along the lip of the gorge. At higher flows the rapids wash out and become a little easier, but the speed and gradient of the water rushing through this gorge and the boils at the end may surprise the unwary paddler.

From below Dulsie Bridge there are some easier Grade 2 – 3 rapids taking you down below Glenferness House high on the right (937429). As the river takes a left-hand bend it enters a scenic steep-sided gorge of vertical rock topped with woodland. This section can be viewed from the road that runs on the north side of the river. The first rapid in this gorge is a tricky Grade 4, easy to recognise as the river drops away to the left against a rockwall. Inspection is easy on the right-hand rock beds and care must be taken in choosing a line that avoids crashing into a midstream rock below the drop. Following this are a series of Grade 3 rapids with powerful stoppers to avoid in high water. A small chapel is passed on the right and high above on the hill is an old bell tower. The gorge now mellows out into Grade 2 – 3 rapids before reaching the A939 road bridge below Ferness (960462).

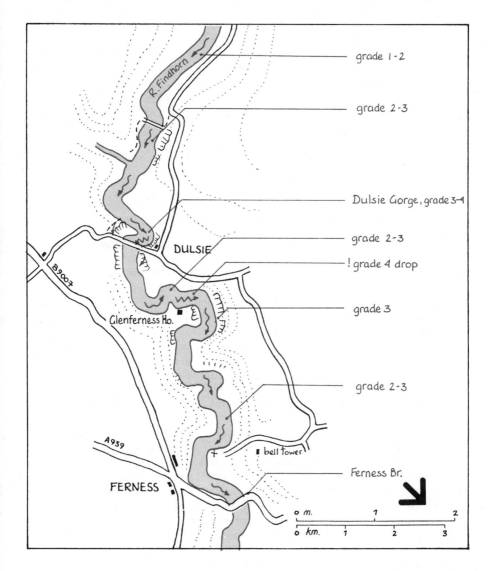

Ferness Bridge to Randolf's Leap

Start (960462)   Finish (000495)   Grade 3   Distance 4mls/6km

This section is suitable for canoeists wishing to build up their skills for the sections above and below. There are a series of Grade 2 – 3 rapids through wooded scenery and rocky banks culminating in a Grade 3 rapid just above a small stone bridge (986488). A mile below is Randolf's Leap, which is easily recognised by the narrow gap through which the river passes and the tall rock face and large eddy on the right. Get out here to follow a footpath up to the road which passes a small stone commemorating the Great Moray floods of 1829, when the river rose to forty feet above its current level. Do not go through the gap unless you intend to run the lower river or attempt the falls fifty yards further on.

Randolf's Leap to Forres Bridge

Start (000495)   Finish (012581)   Grade 3 – 5   Distance 8mls/13km

Just downstream of the gap are Randolf's Leap Falls. These can be Grade 4+ to Grade 6 depending upon the river levels and your state of mind at the time of inspecting them. The falls can be inspected from the right, in which case it's best to get out before the gap, or from the left by running through the gap and stopping just before the falls. Caution should be exercised as these falls change character considerably with different river levels. They can vary from deep chutes to a mass of boils and anything in between, so inspection is essential on the day to determine the level of risk.

For those wishing to avoid these falls an alternative put-in for the lower section is via a footpath down to the River Divie, a tributary of the Findhorn, or where the road crosses over the River Divie. There are some small rapids to negotiate before you join the Findhorn. The first three miles of this section run into tight narrow gorges with a succession of difficult rapids and drops. The warm-up is on Grade 2 – 3 rapids until you reach Logie House on the right bank.

From Logie House the gorge begins with several Grade 3 – 5 rapids, which on most occasions will require some inspection to check out the routes as there are several nasty stoppers to avoid. In high water this is a high-volume Alpine-style descent and is worth every mile you may have to travel to get here. For the adrenaline junkie the gorge ends far too soon, but beyond this, although the river is generally Grade 2, it is no less spectacular. There are tall, impressive sandstone cliffs, carved and undercut where the river has eaten back through the raised sill of an ancient seashore. It is time to relax a little and to reflect upon the beauty and wildness of the Findhorn before the pubs and cafes of Forres lure you away. This section finishes at Findhorn Bridge (012581) and there is easy access on the right, just before the bridge.

If reaching the sea is your objective, then it's about five miles from Findhorn Bridge to the coastal village of Findhorn at the seaward end of the mud flats of Findhorn Bay.

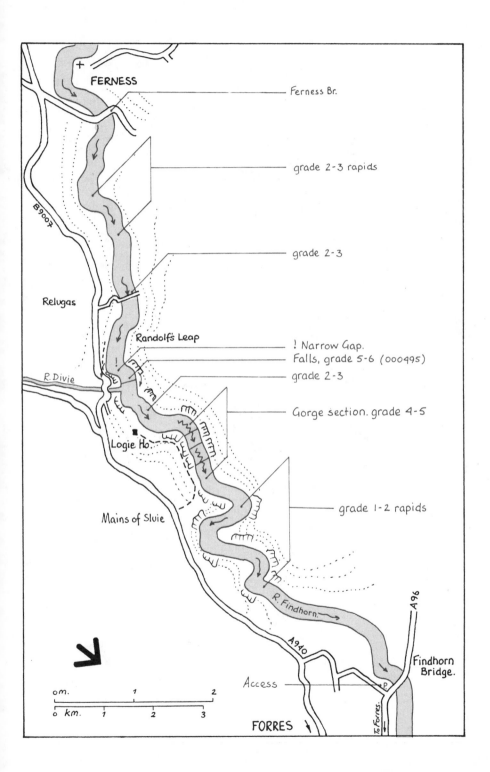

FERNESS

Ferness Br.

grade 2-3 rapids

grade 2-3

B9007

Relugas

Randolf's Leap

! Narrow Gap.
Falls, grade 5-6 (000495)
grade 2-3

R. Divie

Gorge section. grade 4-5

Logie Ho.

Mains of Sluie

grade 1-2 rapids

R. Findhorn.

A96

A940

Findhorn
Bridge.

Access

o m.   1   2

o km.   1   2   3

To Forres

FORRES

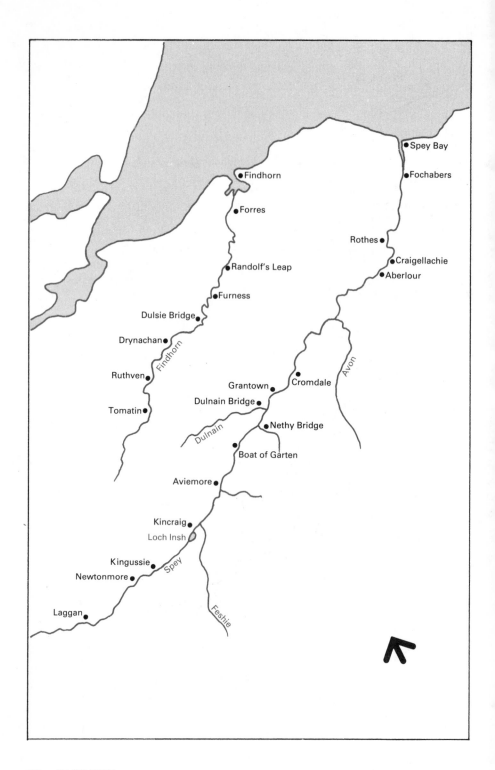

RIVER SPEY

Loch Insh to Fochabers

OS Sheets 28/35/36   62½mls/100km   Grade 2

The Spey is regarded as Britain's fastest flowing river. The name Spey is derived from the Gaelic 'speidh', meaning strength or speed. At Spey Bay, where the Spey flows into the North Sea, the power and volume of the river is sufficient to keep the tides from pushing more than half a mile inland. The Spey is canoeable for almost its entire length and there is usually sufficient water, even in the summer months, to give excellent sport through beautiful scenery, a factor that has made it one of the most popular canoe touring rivers in Scotland.

From its source, high up in the Monadhliath Mountains at Loch Spey, the river collects the water of many mountain streams and by the time it reaches Newtonmore it is already broad and swift.

The Spey Valley is formed by the imposing masses of the Monadhliaths on the left and the Cairngorms on the right. Several major tributaries join the Spey along its length, ensuring that the flow of the river is maintained, and some of these, the Feshie, Dulnain and Avon, are excellent canoeing rivers in their own right. From Kingussie the Spey flows through open marshy land and then into Loch Insh with its tree-lined shores and wooded islands. From here to Fochabers and even down into Spey Bay there are more than sixty miles of river from which to choose, either for a day's canoe trip or even a multi-day expedition. The rapids are rarely more than Grade 2 in difficulty and are usually long, fast and bouncy, with plenty of waves, providing scope for paddlers of all abilities whether in canoes or kayaks.

Speyside is not just popular with canoeists, it has become a prime tourist area with a fast road linking it to Inverness, Edinburgh and Glasgow. For fishermen, the Spey is perhaps at the top of the list of Scotland's best salmon fishing rivers and you will see many small fishing huts and lodges along its banks. It is a busy river during the fishing season, despite the high cost of permits, and, as on other rivers, consideration and courtesy should be shown on passing a fisherman and care should be taken to paddle quietly through fishing pools. Aviemore has become the focal point of winter skiing in Britain, and the Cairngorms and surrounding mountains provide unlimited opportunities for hill walking and climbing. Speyside is also renowned for one other item – whisky. Its distilleries, and the malts they produce, are world famous – maybe that is another reason why the Spey is so popular with canoeists!

Access considerations on the River Spey
Refer to the section 'Access in Scotland' on Page 9.

Loch Insh to Grantown

*Start (838045)   Finish (033269)   Grade 1 – 2   Distance 23mls/37km (Loch Insh to Aviemore 7mls/11km
Aviemore to Boat of Garten 7mls/11km   Boat of Garten to Grantown 9mls/15km)*

Nestled between the Monadhliath Mountains to the west and the Cairngorm wilderness
to the east, the marshy land above Loch Insh has been designated a Site of Special
Scientific Interest for its distinctive flora and fauna and for its breeding of wintering
wildfowl. For the canoeist this upper part of the river is open and exposed; however, it
does offer fine views of the surrounding mountains. At Loch Insh the woodland comes
down to the shoreline and on the eastern shore is the Loch Insh Watersports Centre,
ideally situated for all forms of watersports: sailing, windsurfing and of course
canoeing, offering expeditions and whitewater courses for all levels on the River Spey.
From Loch Insh the river flows around a large wooded island and down to the bridge at
Kincraig. Half a mile further on the River Feshie enters from the right, and this is also a
popular river amongst whitewater canoeists, with a tricky Grade 3 – 4 gorge a couple of
miles upstream at Feshiebridge. The Spey, however, maintains its level at Grade 1 – 2,
passing occasional shingle banks where the constricted flow forces the pace of the river.
In the distance you will see the Duke of Gordon's monument, a tall column on a hillock to
the left.

At Aviemore, seven miles from Loch Insh, there is access to the river between the
two bridges. To the west of Aviemore is the Rothiemurchus estate which lies between
the Spey and the high ground of the Cairngorms. Low-lying fields and hardwoods on
the river flood-plain give way to open heather moorland, birch woods, forestry
plantations and the last remnants of the once vast Caledonian pine forest. This estate
has been a National Nature Reserve since 1954 and it offers a whole range of activities
from nature walks to fishing and shooting.

From Aviemore the flood plain opens out and there are occasional small rapids
building up in volume as the river nears Boat of Garten. There is another nature reserve
to the west of Boat of Garten at Loch Garten. This one is famous for its ospreys which
return each spring from their winter quarters in Africa. From the first recolonisation by
one pair in the 1950s over fifty young ospreys have flown from the Loch Garten Reserve.

For the next few miles from Boat of Garten the odd shingle rapid breaks up the slow
flat water. Below Nethy Bridge the River Dulnain flows in from the left; this too is a
canoeable tributary from above Carrbridge. The wooded slopes close in again as you
near Grantown-on-Spey and there is easy access on the left before the road bridge.

Note: Canoe courses and boat hire are available at: Loch Insh Watersports Centre,
Insh Hall, Kincraig PH21 1NU (☎ 05404 272)

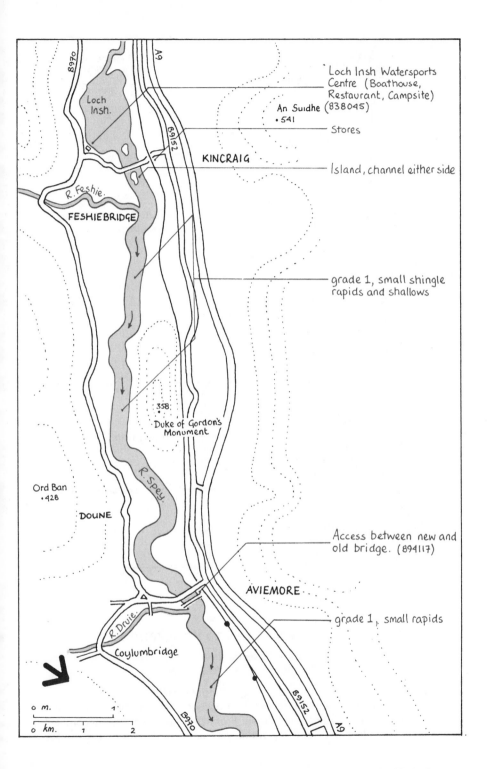

Loch Insh Watersports
Centre (Boathouse,
Restaurant, Campsite)
(838045)

An Suidhe
• 541

Stores

Island, channel either side

Loch
Insh.

KINCRAIG

R.Feshie

FESHIEBRIDGE

grade 1, small shingle
rapids and shallows

358
Duke of Gordon's
Monument

R.Spey.

Ord Ban
• 428

DOUNE

Access between new and
old bridge. (894117)

AVIEMORE

R.Druie

Coylumbridge

grade 1, small rapids

o m.   1
o km.   1   2

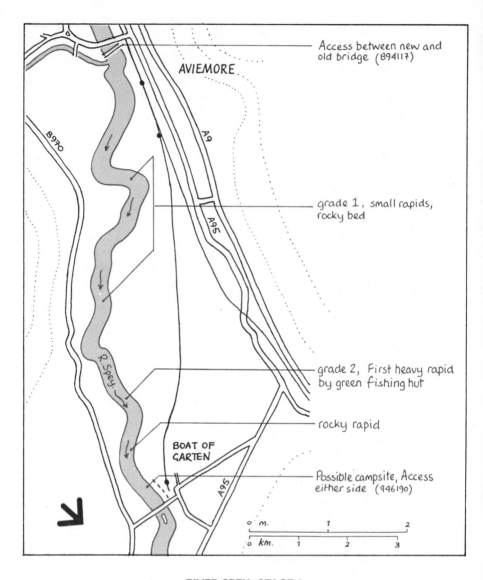

Access between new and old bridge (894117)

AVIEMORE

grade 1, small rapids, rocky bed

grade 2, First heavy rapid by green fishing hut

rocky rapid

BOAT OF GARTEN

Possible campsite, Access either side (946190)

R. Spey

B970

A9

A95

A95

o m.   1   2
o km.   1   2   3

RIVER SPEY: STAGE 2

Grantown-on-Spey to Knockando

Start (033269)   Finish (192417)   Grade 1   Distance 18mls/29km (Grantown to Advie 10½mls/17km Advie to Knockando 7½mls/12km)

Grantown-on-Spey was built as a result of an enterprising laird, Grant of Grant, who laid out the plans for a new town in 1765 to encourage workers to settle there. Its grid-like street system has altered little since then. From Grantown the river becomes more scenic with the valley-sides closing in and obscuring the views of the mountains.

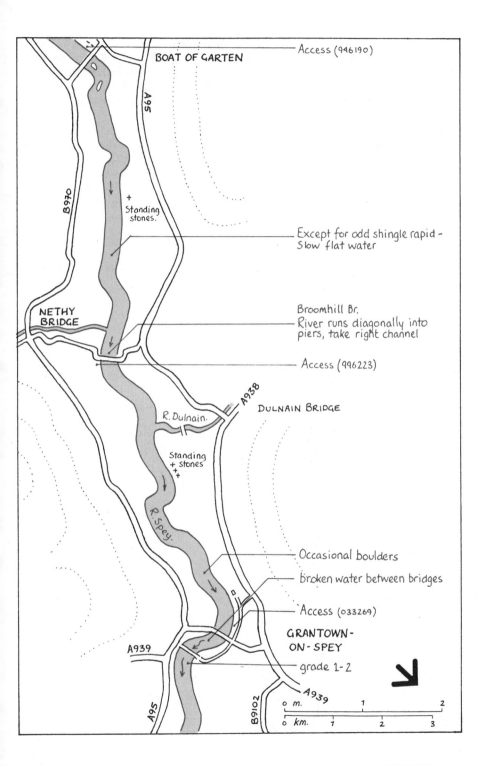

BOAT OF GARTEN

Access (946190)

A95

B970

Standing stones.

Except for odd shingle rapid - Slow flat water

NETHY BRIDGE

Broomhill Br.
River runs diagonally into piers, take right channel

Access (996223)

A938

R. Dulnain.

DULNAIN BRIDGE

Standing stones

R. Spey.

Occasional boulders

broken water between bridges

Access (033269)

GRANTOWN-ON-SPEY

A939

grade 1-2

A939

A95

B9102

| o m. | | 1 | | 2 |
| o km. | 1 | 2 | 3 |

Between the two bridges there are rocky rapids with a notable Grade 2 just by the old bridge. To the west the river is flanked by the Hills of Cromdale, it now provides more entertaining rapids. This stretch is also popular for fishing and you will pass many secluded fishing lodges on the river banks as you near Knockando.

Below Advie Bridge begins one of the most popular canoeing runs on the Spey. If you have come up for the whitewater on the surrounding rivers and the levels are too low then this stretch is well worth a paddle for its fast and long Grade 2 rapids. There is convenient access below Advie where the B9102 runs close to the river on the left. At Ballindalloch there is a hostel offering self-catering accommodation, details of which are available from Loch Insh Watersports Centre. Ballindalloch also marks the end of the

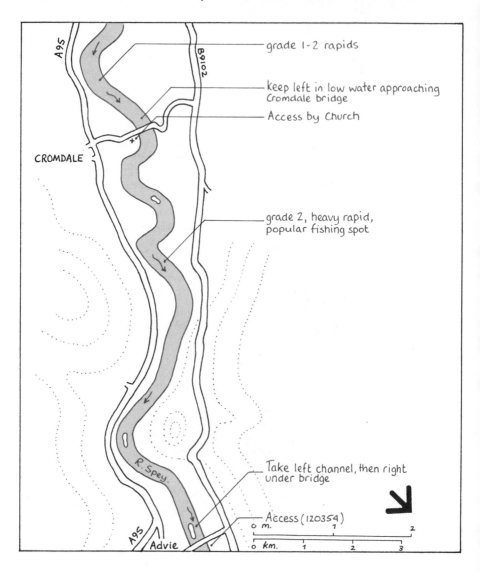

grade 1-2 rapids

keep left in low water approaching Cromdale bridge

Access by Church

CROMDALE

grade 2, heavy rapid, popular fishing spot

R. Spey.

Take left channel, then right under bridge

Access (120354)

o m.   1   2

o km.   1   2   3

A95

B9102

A95

Advie

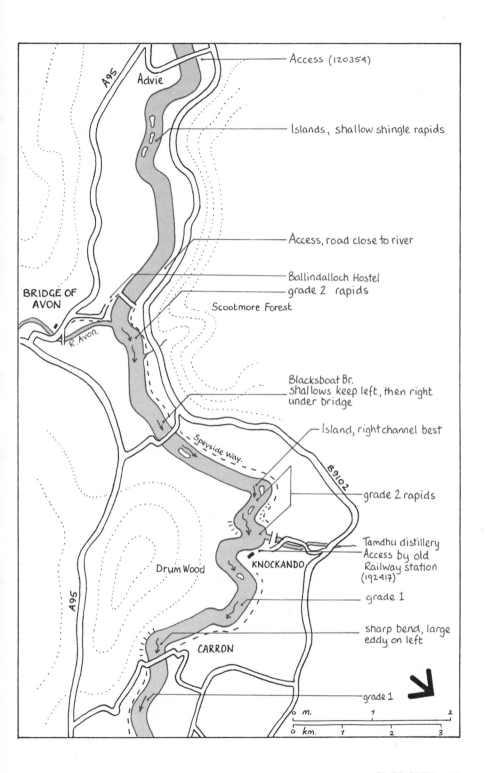

Access (120354)

Islands, shallow shingle rapids

Access, road close to river

Ballindalloch Hostel
grade 2 rapids

Scootmore Forest

Blacksboat Br.
shallows keep left, then right
under bridge

Island, right channel best

grade 2 rapids

Tamdhu distillery
Access by old
Railway station
(192417)

grade 1

sharp bend, large
eddy on left

grade 1

A95

Advie

BRIDGE OF
AVON

R. Avon.

Speyside Way

B9102

Drum Wood

KNOCKANDO

A95

CARRON

o m.   1   2
o km.   1   2   3

current extent of the Speyside Way, a long-distance footpath running from Spey Bay following footpaths, minor roads and disused railway lines. There is a spur of the route to Tomintoul and it is hoped to extend the walk to Glenmore.

Between the old railway bridge at Ballindalloch and Knockando there are plenty of rapids to keep you busy. A sharp left-hand bend with a steep bank on the right brings you to the start of the Knockando rapids. As you round the corner the Tamdhu distillery can be seen and before this there are a couple of ledge rapids to negotiate. Immediately below these rapids it is possible to exit on the left where a path takes you up to the old Tamdhu station which is now used as a Visitors' Centre for the distillery.

The Tamdhu distillery produces one of the many famous malts in Scotland and its distinctive peaty flavour is infused with the whisky by smoking the barley over burning peat. This distillery is one of seven included in the 'Only Malt Whisky Trail in the World' a seventy-mile tour by car of the Strathiola, Glenfiddich, Tarmavilin, Glenlivet, Glenfarclas, Tamdhu and Glengrant distilleries, although I'm not sure if you are meant to do them all in one day!

Note: To book in at Ballindolloch Hostel telephone Insh Hall, Kincraig ☎ 05404 272.

RIVER SPEY: STAGE 3

Knockando to Fochabers

Start (192417)   Finish (342595)   Grade 1 – 2   Distance 21½mls/35km (Knockando to Craigellachie 8½mls/13½km   Craigellachie to Boat o' Brig 8mls/13km   Boat o' Brig to Fochabers 5mls/8km   Fochabers to Tugnet 4mls/6½km)

From the access point below Tamdhu distillery take the river onwards past several bends and then through a narrow valley with forested slopes on the right, the interest maintained with plenty of small rapids and the occasional island. After a long straight reach of a mile the river takes a sharp bend to the left and passes under Carron Bridge. A track on the left, beyond the bridge, leads back to the road. The valley widens but the rapids persist until the town of Aberlour is approached just after the Victoria Suspension Bridge. Its full name is Charlestown of Aberlour, and it was established in 1812 by Charles Grant, one of three brothers who developed towns; the other towns, also named eponymously, being Archiestown and Robertstown a few miles to the west. A long straight stretch of river takes you towards Craigellachie. Here the Spey is spanned by a bridge built by Thomas Telford in 1815, which is one of the few that survived the great floods in 1829, yet another reminder of his genius as an engineer. Nestling on the right between the Telford Bridge and the modern road bridge there is a discreet campsite.

A few miles downstream from Craigellachie is Rothes and beyond that the river leaves the hill country as the land opens out to the west. On the right, steep hillsides still keep the river on its northerly course. It is now wide and there are many shallows and large islands. Before you reach Fochabers you will pass the Earth Pillars of Ordiequish on the right – tall red needles of Old Red Sandstone conglomerate left behind as the softer earth around was gradually washed away.

There is an access point at Fochabers just below the second bridge on the right. From

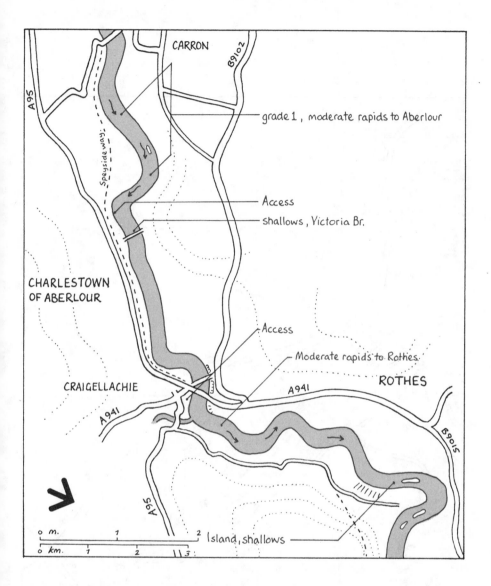

CARRON

B9102

grade 1 , moderate rapids to Aberlour

A95

Speyside way.

Access

shallows , Victoria Br.

CHARLESTOWN OF ABERLOUR

Access

Moderate rapids to Rothes.

ROTHES

CRAIGELLACHIE

A941

A941

B9015

A95

Island, shallows

o m.   1   2
o km.   1   2   3

here it is a further four miles down to Spey Bay, through shifting shingle banks and under the old railway viaduct and finally to Tugnet at the mouth of the Spey. If you paddle this last stretch, finish at the Old Ice House at Tugnet. This was built to store the winter ice which, in the insulated chambers, lasted throughout the season and was used to pack the freshly caught salmon for their journey towards London. The Ice House now contains an exhibition of the life and work of the Settlement of Tugnet.

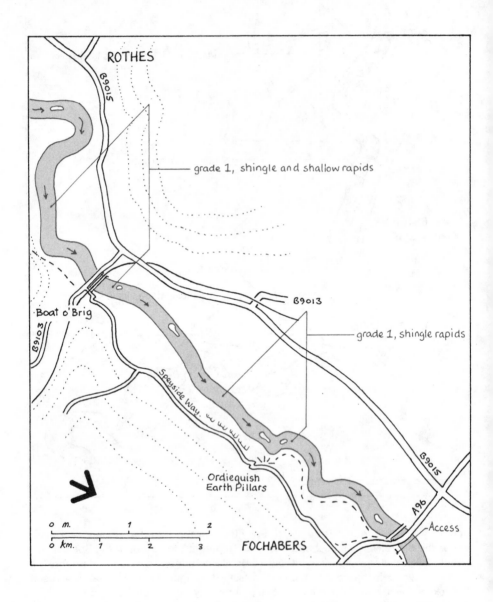

ROTHES

B9015

grade 1, shingle and shallow rapids

Boat o' Brig

B9103

B9013

grade 1, shingle rapids

Speyside Way

B9015

Ordiequish
Earth Pillars

A96

Access

o m. 1 2

o km. 1 2 3

FOCHABERS

RIVER ORCHY

LOCH TULLA TO LOCH AWE

OS Sheet 50   16½ miles/26½km   Grade 3 – 5

The River Orchy begins as the outflow from Loch Tulla, which itself is fed by the waters that run down from the heights of the Black Mount and from the wilderness of Rannoch Moor. The river flows for twelve miles through the beautiful Glen Orchy: in its upper half bounded by the slopes of Beinn Udlaidh and Ben Inverveigh with its extensive forests on the western side; at the lower end hemmed in between Beinn na Sroine and Beinn Donachain, after which it is joined by the River Lochy. From this confluence the river continues a few more miles through the Strath of Orchy before emptying into the great expanse of Loch Awe.

The River Orchy with its high concentration of rapids and falls has understandably gained the reputation of being one of the best whitewater canoeing rivers in the country. At low to medium levels its rapids are suitable for the competent canoeist wishing to gain further whitewater experience, but when the river is full the power and the volume of the rapids increase dramatically, providing a challenging run for even the most skilled canoeist. The best introductory sections are on the upper and lower parts of the river where one can perfect the skills of whitewater canoeing amidst magnificent surroundings.

The river is easily accessible from the B8074 which runs parallel to it through Glen Orchy. A gauge on the Bridge of Orchy allows the river's level to be checked. Two feet on the gauge equates with a medium level. Above three feet the rapids can increase by a full grade of difficulty.

For those of you who have arrived hoping to find the Orchy in high water but are faced with a dry bed of rocks, then drive further north across Rannoch Moor and turn off into Glen Etive to check out the numerous splendid waterfalls on the River Etive that will have some eagerly preparing for their boats and others rushing off to the nearest bar.

Access considerations for the River Orchy
Refer to section 'Access in Scotland' on Page 9.

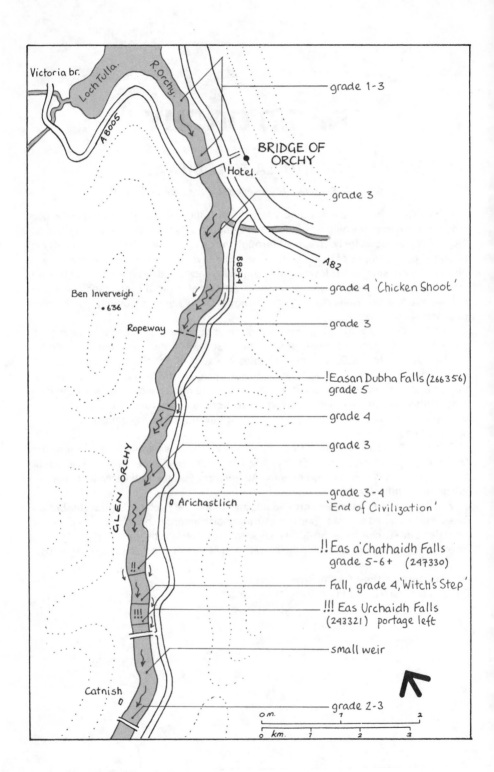

grade 1-3

BRIDGE OF ORCHY

Hotel.

grade 3

A82

grade 4 'Chicken Shoot'

grade 3

!Easan Dubha Falls (266356) grade 5

grade 4

grade 3

grade 3-4 'End of Civilization'

!! Eas a'Chathaidh Falls grade 5-6+ (247330)

Fall, grade 4, 'Witch's Step'

!!! Eas Urchaidh Falls (243321) portage left

small weir

grade 2-3

Victoria br.

Loch Tulla

R. Orchy

A8005

Ben Inverveigh
• 636

Ropeway

GLEN ORCHY

Arichastlich

Catnish

B8074

0 m.   1   2

0   km.   1   2   3

Loch Tulla to Easan Dubha Falls

Start (293420) *Finish (267357)* **Grade** *3 – 4 (Easan Dubha Falls 4 – 5)* **Distance** *5mls/7½km*

From Loch Tulla to Bridge of Orchy the river flows at a steady pace with Grade 1 – 2 rapids which, with more water, can reach Grade 3. It is easy to inspect this section from the road on the west side of the river. An alternative starting-point to extend the section can be at Victoria Bridge (271422) which crosses Linne-nam-Beathach, a tributary river flowing into Loch Tulla at its western end, but the owner has asked that this start is not used during the fishing season.

From Bridge of Orchy to the start of Glen Orchy there are Grade 2 rapids but this changes when the B8074 moves closer to the river. At this point there is a Grade 3 rapid with a large central rock. This section is an ideal introduction to the Orchy and those canoeists who do not want to push things any further can exit here and retire to the Bridge of Orchy Hotel for refreshment.

As the river continues down Glen Orchy the next major obstacle is a Grade 4 rapid known as 'Chicken Shoot'. This will need inspection to determine which route to take to avoid the rocks at the end. It may be portaged on either bank. A Grade 3 rapid that follows tends to channel the canoeist down into a hole on the right which, in good conditions, can provide an excellent playspot. Just below this a cableway crosses over the river and it has been known for canoeists to ferry themselves and their boats out to the centre of the river in the 'bucket' and to seal launch into the river.

After the cableway another mile of easy rapids brings you to Easan Dubha, the first big fall on the river. This Grade 5 fall may be inspected or portaged on the left-hand bank as the road is close at hand. Recirculating boils and a powerful stopper can make the fall a very hazardous proposition. Spectators should be wary of the slippery rocks by the fall or they may well end up joining the canoeists in the river.

Easan Dubha to Falls of Orchy

Start (267357) *Finish (243321)* **Grade** *3 – 5 (two portages)* **Distance** *3½mls/5km*

This is the most severe section of the Orchy with many rapids and falls which provide an endless challenge to the whitewater canoeist. Immediately below Easan Dubha is a wide and long Grade 4 rapid and care should be taken to avoid the long stopper that forms in higher flows and the many sharp rocks that lie beneath the surface. Fortunately like all the rapids on this section it is easy to inspect or portage. Grade 3 rapids follow leading into 'End of Civilisation', a long Grade 4 rapid of wide ledges and stoppers.

By now you will be well into the rapids on this section but don't forget that a little further on lies Eas a'Chathaidh (247330), a large and dangerous fall (Grade 5 – 6+) that stretches across the river. Get out in good time to inspect. At most levels the river divides around a central island, taking a straight drop on the right and a stepped drop on

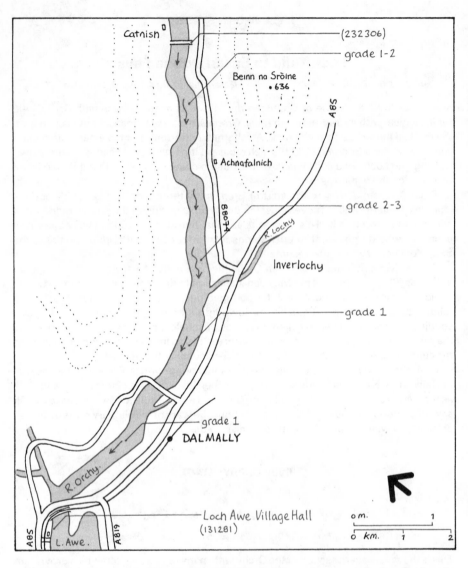

Catnish □ ─────────────── (232306)
─────────── grade 1-2

Beinn na Sròine
● 636

A85

□ Achnafalnich

B8074 ─────── grade 2-3

R. Lochy

Inverlochy

─────── grade 1

grade 1
● DALMALLY

R. Orchy.

A85

A819

Loch Awe Village Hall
(131281)

L. Awe.

0 m. ─────────── 1
0 km. ──── 1 ──── 2

the left. It may be contemplated in certain levels but if you have any doubts the drop is best portaged.

A short distance beyond Eas a'Chathaidh the road meets with the river again and drops over 'Witch's Step', a Grade 4 ledge where inspection is also essential to determine the best route. From here it is easy going until Eas Urchaidh, the Falls of Orchy (243321). It is best to exit on the left bank above these falls as the trench-shaped gully into which the river flows, with its undercut rocks and scour holes is definitely an uninviting prospect.

Falls of Orchy to Loch Awe

Start (243321)   Finish (131281)   Grade 1 – 3   Distance 8½mls/14km

For those canoeists who prefer an easier whitewater run without the fear of being swept uncontrollably down thundering rapids, this section of the Lower Orchy below Eas Urchaidh is ideal. It begins with a small weir and continues with several Grade 2 – 3 rapids to the footbridge at Catnish (232306). The river calms down for a few miles before reaching some more Grade 2 – 3 rapids over rock ledges.

After the confluence with the River Lochy the Orchy calms down for the final run down to Loch Awe, finally entering the lake after passing under the road and rail bridge. There is a take-out at Loch Awe Village Hall on the right (131281).

Loch Awe is drained by the River Awe flowing through the Pass of Brander. This is a dam-controlled river and from below the barrage (045287) to Loch Etive there is a good Grade 3 run before some dangerous weirs are reached, which may need portage.

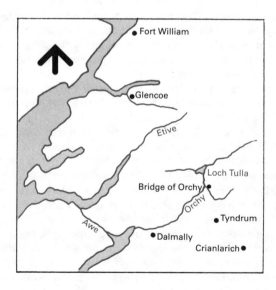

RIVER WYE

LLANGURIG TO CHEPSTOW

OS Sheets 147/148/149/161/162   147 miles/241km   Grade 2 – 3 (upper river)   1 – 2 (lower river)

The source of the Wye can be found near the peak of Plynlimon, in mid-Wales. Plynlimon the 'Watery Mountain' gives rise to three rivers: the Wye, the Rheidol and the Severn. The Wye and Severn take diverse routes away from the mountain only to meet again in the Severn estuary at Chepstow. Unlike the Severn, the Wye, in the course of its descent, has avoided areas of industrial development; this has kept it free from pollution so that its rural river system maintains a wide range of plant and animal life. Because of this the Wye has gained an enviable reputation as one of Britain's most beautiful and unspoilt rivers.

The scenery of the Wye owes much to its geological history. Millions of years ago the area was a vast river delta depositing sands and silts washed down from the mountains to the north. Later it became a warm sea and the shells of countless sea creatures were deposited to become limestones. As the sea-level fell the Wye began to cut downwards through these rock levels. The Old Red Sandstones form the gentler sloping valleys, while the limestones were eroded to form the precipitous gorges and cliffs of Yat Rocks, Seven Sisters' Rocks, Shorn Cliff, Wyndcliffe and Wintour's Leap.

The Wye has influenced the life of its inhabitants since prehistory, when early man sheltered in the caves of the lower Wye and its course as a natural border gave rise to castles and fortifications. Twelve hundred years ago, Offa, King of Mercia, built his Dyke, a rampart from the mouth of the Wye to the Dee, traces of which remain today and are now linked by a long-distance footpath.

Early industry developed on the lower Wye as coal and iron ore were mined in the Forest of Dean, and soon river traffic became extremely important as the Wye established itself as a commercial waterway.

Despite various schemes to improve navigation, river traffic still had to depend on the tides and the amount of water in the river. Sailing vessels were able to sail from Chepstow to Brockweir, the limit of tidal water. From here goods were unloaded onto barges to continue to Ross or Hereford. Since the sixteenth century the Wye from Chepstow to Hay has been a free navigation as a result of its commercialisation. This however does not imply a right of access to the river bank across private land.

In the late eighteenth century the River Wye began to develop a tourist trade as it became fashionable amongst the upper classes to experience the 'Wye Tour', a boat journey on the lower Wye. The scenery of this area attracted many artists and poets of the time who enthused about its charms through pen and brush. By 1827 several boats a day were leaving Ross and making the journey to Chepstow with an overnight stop at Monmouth. The tourer travelled in style, in awning-covered boats and with good food and wine. This tourist trade continued for more than a hundred years and a guide to the Wye Valley, written in 1903, described a boat journey from Hay to Chepstow. In those days the cost of a boat trip from Hereford to Chepstow, including an oarsman and cartage back to Hereford, was seventy-five shillings. The 'Wye Tour' appears to be no more, unless someone is enterprising enough to revive the luxury river tours with hotel and champagne stops.

In the nineteenth century, due to the failing ore deposits, industry declined and river traffic switched to the Hereford and Gloucester Canal which was opened in 1845, and the Wye began to restore itself to its previous natural beauty.

Except for the few short-distance pleasure-boat trips available today it is the canoe that has become the most popular craft on the river.

For canoeists the river can be navigated from as high up as Llangurig. This section of river down to the start of the navigation at Hay is under private ownership and may be subject to access agreements. The upper Wye provides several stretches of river with rapids from Grade 2 to 3 and it has become a popular venue for whitewater tourers. The lower Wye still retains its reputation for canoe touring through an area of outstanding natural beauty and there are several places on the river where canoes can be hired or canoe trips undertaken with guides and instructors.

As well as being popular with canoeists the Wye is also well-known for both game and coarse fishing. The cleanliness of the river has created an ideal environment for salmon and it is famed as one of Britain's best salmon fishing rivers. On the lower river where the right of navigation exists there is no conflict with anglers and none should arise if you are considerate and courteous, passing through fishing pools quickly and quietly or passing behind fishing boats on the river. On the upper Wye where the river is under private ownership and the fishing rights are owned by angling associations, conflict has arisen in the mistaken belief that canoeing disturbs fishing, a strange idea considering the situation on the lower river.

Access considerations on the River Wye

The river below Hay-on-Wye is an ancient right of navigation; however, this does not imply a right of access to the river across private land for launching or landing, where permission must be gained in advance.

The upper Wye above Hay-on-Wye is subject to access agreements and the access position should be ascertained before any trip. Full details of access points and agreements are available from the Local Access Officer (WCA).

Note: For general location map of the River Wye see page 125.

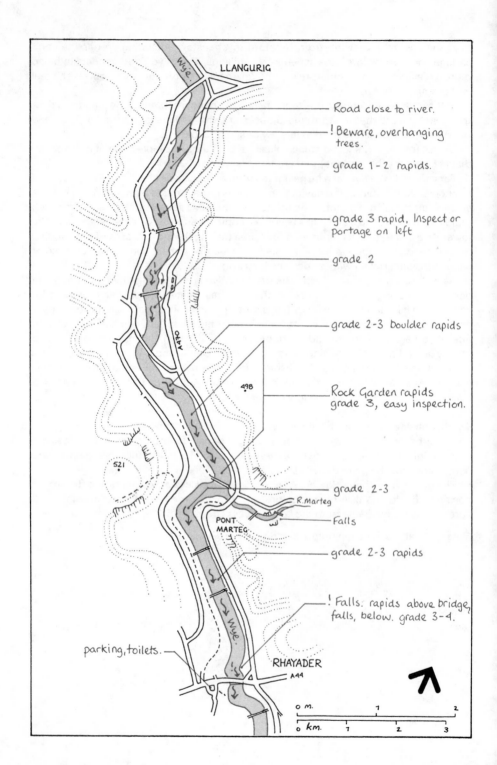

LLANGURIG

Road close to river.

! Beware, overhanging trees.

grade 1-2 rapids.

grade 3 rapid, Inspect or portage on left

grade 2

grade 2-3 boulder rapids

Rock Garden rapids grade 3, easy inspection.

grade 2-3

R.Marteg

Falls

PONT MARTEG

grade 2-3 rapids

! Falls: rapids above bridge, falls below. grade 3-4.

parking, toilets.

RHAYADER

A44

498

521

Wye.

Wye.

Wye.

o m.   1   2

o km.   1   2   3

Llangurig to Rhayader

*Start (908797)   Finish (968679)   Grade 3 (Rhayader Falls 3 – 4)   Distance 10mls/15km
(Llangurig to Marteg 7mls/11km   Marteg to Rhayader 3mls/5km)*

The Wye from Llangurig to Rhayader provides one of the most popular and exciting whitewater runs in the region. The upper Wye from Llangurig to Glasbury is under private ownership and details of any access agreements currently operating should be obtained in advance from the Access Officer for the Wye. This top section of river is a prime fishing spot and spawning ground and is usually too rocky to make a worthwhile descent in low-water conditions. Medium to high levels are best when the rapids have sufficient volume to make them entertaining without the fear of grounding or rock-bashing.

From Llangurig the river runs gently through a wide valley. Occasionally the banks on either side are lined with overhanging trees, a hazard that requires special caution in high water. The first major rapid is encountered on a sharp left-hand corner. It can be inspected from the left bank. At this point the river constricts into a narrow channel through the bedrock and flows into a vertical headwall with an enclosed eddy on the right. From here small rapids and swift water carry you down to a concrete road bridge (922738), an alternative starting point.

Below the concrete bridge the valley begins to narrow and the river becomes studded with rocks requiring intricate manoeuvres. Another hazard to watch out for on the next stretch are fallen trees. Soon the river enters the gorge section and the banks steepen into woodland and moss-covered rocks. Although the channels remain generally wide the routes are not always obvious from the boat, this section is more like a giant slalom course. A major fall known as the 'Rock Garden' occurs in this section. It is a tricky rapid running left to right and care is needed to avoid unwelcome rocks. Rescue cover is fortunately easy on this section. A few more chutes carry you down to the Marteg confluence (952715) and a footbridge across the river.

The Marteg, flowing in from the left, appears to be a shallow, rocky, mountain stream. However, half a mile up stream of the confluence is an excellent gorge section (Grade 5) that is worth a look and is runnable in medium to high water levels if you so wish. From the confluence there are several Grade 2 and 3 rapids, the most notable occurring by the old railway bridge abutments a little further on. This scenic run, past tree-lined banks, ends by the caravan park on the left as you near Rhayader town.

At Rhayader, by its full name Rhayader-gwy, 'Fall of the Wye', the river rushes down to the road bridge. Immediately beneath the bridge begins Rhayader Falls (Grade 3 – 4). Usually there is a calm section above, where you can stop to view the choice of routes. The central route has a vicious corkscrewing current and it is best to run left or right of this. Beyond the bridge there is a brief respite in which to decide your next option – either a straight drop to the right or the easier salmon steps to the left. In either case the river converges below into a narrow gap on the right, after which it opens out. The trip can finish here for the car-park, cafes and pubs of Rhayader or for a quick break before continuing to Llanwrthwl or Newbridge. If you finish here, then take a drive up the Elan valley to view the reservoirs and to check out some interesting sections of rivers that connect them.

Rhayader to Builth Wells

Start (968679)   *Finish (042511)*   *Grade 2 – 3*   *Distance 16mls/26km (Rhayader to Llanwrthwl 4mls/6km   Llanwrthwl to Newbridge 5mls/8km   Newbridge to Builth Wells 8mls/13km)*

From Rhayader Falls there are several small Grade 2 rapids leading down to Railway Rapids, a Grade 3 run beneath an old railway bridge, before the confluence with the Afon Elan. It is wise to inspect this for it can be a rocky and difficult run in low water and it

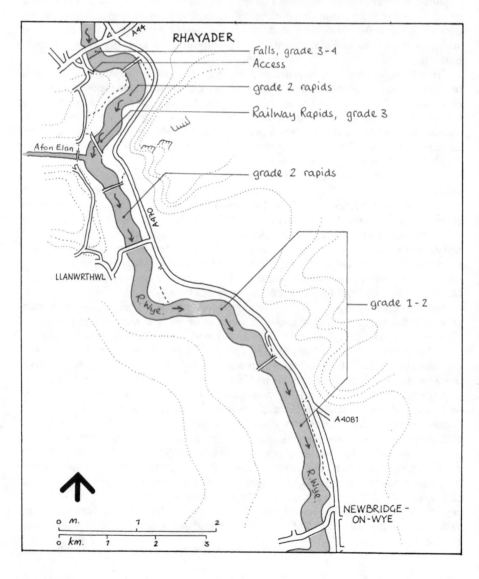

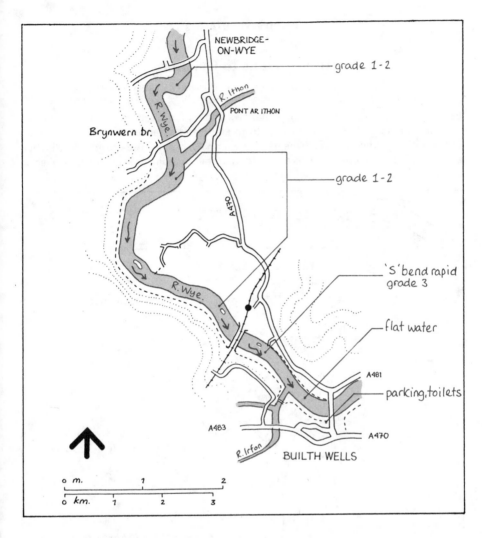

NEWBRIDGE-
ON-WYE

grade 1-2

R. Ithon

PONT AR ITHON

Brynwern br.

R. Wye

A470

grade 1-2

'S' bend rapid
grade 3

R. Wye

flat water

A481

parking, toilets

A483

A470

R. Irfon

BUILTH WELLS

o m.   1   2

o km.   1   2   3

produces severe stoppers in high water.

The next few miles are contained between steep banks and there are occasional Grade 2 rapids. Llanwrthwl Bridge is often used as a convenient stopping point for an extended run on the upper Wye, either from Llangurig or from the Marteg confluence. Between Llanwrthwl and Newbridge there are small rapids and shallows.

At Newbridge another popular run commences as there are several rapids on this section of river down to Builth Wells. After Brynwern Bridge (011566) the Ithon flows in on the left, another considerable tributary. Several Grade 2 rapids occur between here and the 'S' bend, a tricky Grade 3 rapid a mile or so before Builth is reached. Here the river is channelled to the right below steep banks and there is a small drop on a tight bend. In high levels the drop tends to wash out but it still remains tricky due to unpredictable currents and boils. The final run to Builth Wells is generally calm and can be slow in low water. Exit above the bridge on the right by the car-park and toilets.

Builth Wells to Glasbury

Start (042511)   Finish (179394)   Grade 2 – 3   Distance 17mls/28km (Builth Wells to Erwood 8mls/13km   Erwood to Boughrood 5mls/8km   Boughrood to Glasbury 4mls/7km)

Below Builth Bridge there are some shallows and rapids (Grade 1 – 2). The country is open but this soon changes as the river turns south and is flanked by steep valley sides and woodland. Where the A470 meets the river on the right bank there are some laybys and these are sometimes used as an alternative starting point to avoid the two miles or

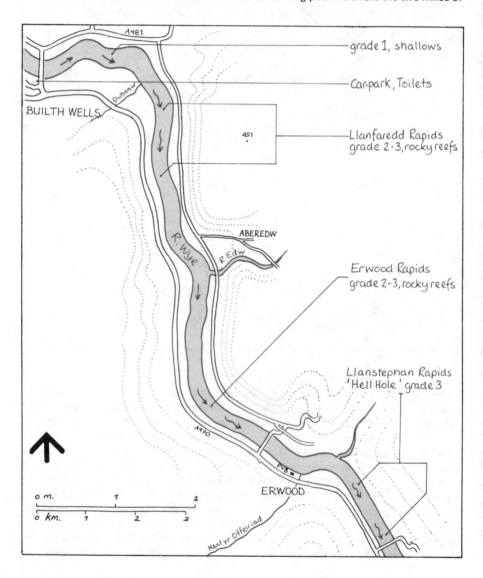

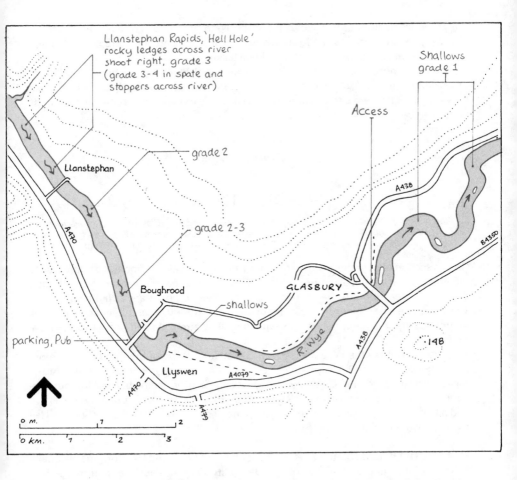

Llanstephan Rapids, 'Hell Hole'
rocky ledges across river
shoot right, grade 3
(grade 3-4 in spate and
stoppers across river)

Shallows
grade 1

Access

grade 2

Llanstephan

grade 2-3

Boughrood

shallows

GLASBURY

parking, Pub

Llyswen

A4079

R. Wye

·148

A470

A438

A470

A479

A438

B4350

0 m.   1   2
0 km.   1   2   3

so from Builth Wells. This popular stretch of river contains three major rapids, all rocky at low water but good Grade 2 – 3 at medium to high levels. The first is Llanfaredd rapids, a half-mile section of rocky reefs. A mile and a half further down, the River Edw flows in from the left. This small narrow river passes through a deep wooded gorge with many fallen trees and small rapids and finishes in a final Grade 3 rapid, under the rail and road bridge, just before converging with the Wye.

The second set of rapids is above Erwood. Again, more rock reefs at low water with an obvious channel through, and in medium to high water a bouncy ride down.

Below Erwood Bridge the Nant-y-offeriad flows in from the right. It ends in a small four-foot fall before it joins the Wye. If you are driving past Erwood it is worth stopping to have a look at the narrow gorge that this river flows through. Runnable in spate from higher up, where it is no more than a drainage ditch, it flows through a deep valley with many rapids and falls. Do not attempt it in lower water as it is a salmon spawning tributary. Below Erwood begins one of the more famous rapids on the Wye, the infamous 'Hell Hole'. This section begins as Llanstephan Bridge comes into sight and as the river flows over rocky reefs that slope upstream. The right-hand channel narrows down to a final chute and stopper which has been responsible for many capsizes over the years. In medium to high flows it is possible to run more centrally over the reefs, however, severe stoppers can form towards the left. In spate there are huge standing waves and long stoppers and care should be taken.

There are more small rapids below Llanstephan Bridge and one final rapid further down where the river runs over a rocky ledge before Boughrood Bridge is reached. Exit here on the right. Between Boughrood and Glasbury there are occasional small rapids which can be shallow in low water.

RIVER WYE: STAGE 4

Glasbury to Hereford

Start (179394) Finish (509396) Grade 1 Distance 36mls/59km (Glasbury to Hay 6mls/10km Hay to Whitney 5mls/8km Whitney to Bredwardine 10mls/16km Bredwardine to Bridge Sollers – Monnington Falls run – 6mls/10km Bridge Sollers to Hereford 9mls/15km)

On this section of river there are many small rapids and shallows, most too numerous to mention. These are usually more evident in low summer conditions and they will soon disappear after a bout of heavy rain when the Wye, fed by many tributaries, can be known to rise at an alarming rate. From Glasbury the river runs between the Black Mountains and the Radnorshire hills with long slow stretches and pools that are ideal for fishing.

Beyond Whitney the Wye crosses the rich pasture lands of the flood plains before again being restricted by high steep banks as it meanders towards Hereford. At the Measllwch Arms Hotel in Glasbury, canoe and kayak trips can be booked for journeys down the river. In the winter months whitewater trips are run on the upper Wye. It is five and a half miles from Glasbury to Hay, with many small rapids. Half a mile before Hay there is a weir, usually run on the right.

There are few hazards on the stretch of river between Hay and Hereford; occasionally there are large boulders in the river, often just below the surface, and just before Whitney Bridge there is debris from a demolished railway bridge. Several islands are passed, usually with one channel less shallow than the other.

The only notable exception to this tranquillity are the Monnington Falls (375429). Almost two miles beyond the high wooded cliff of the 'scar', beyond Bredwardine, the river takes a sharp left-hand bend. It is wise to stop on the left at this point to inspect the river ahead. The falls (Grade 2 – 3) consist of a narrow channel on the left that has cut through the bedrock. In summer conditions the flat bedrocks on the right are usually exposed. The only real hazards are the swirly currents below, which may catch the unwary by surprise.

The final few miles from Monnington to Hereford are usually slow moving and can be arduous in a headwind. At Hereford, land below the old road bridge on the right.

Canoe Hire courses on upper and lower Wye: Maesllwch Arms Hotel, Glasbury, Hereford HR3 5LH (☎ 04974 226)

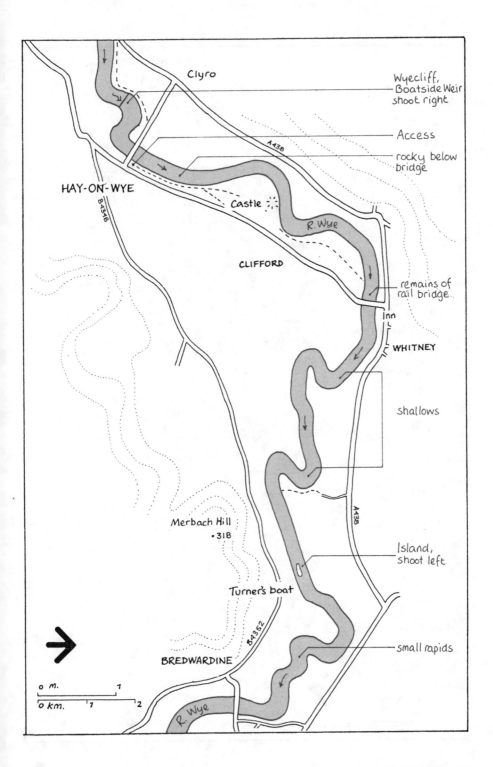

Clyro

Wyecliff,
Boatside Weir
shoot right

Access

A438

rocky below
bridge

HAY-ON-WYE

B4348

Castle

R. Wye

CLIFFORD

remains of
rail bridge

Inn

WHITNEY

shallows

Merbach Hill
•318

A438

Island,
shoot left

Turner's boat

B4352

small rapids

BREDWARDINE

0 m.   1

0 km.   1   2

R. Wye

R. Wye

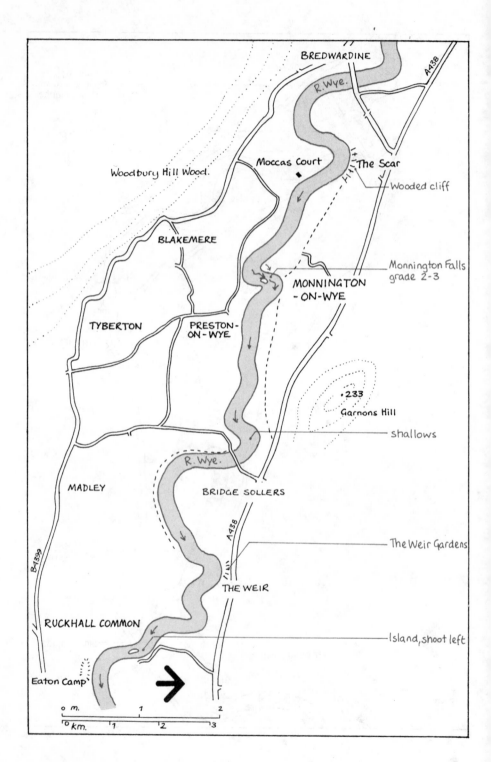

BREDWARDINE

A438

R. Wye.

Woodbury Hill Wood.

Moccas Court

The Scar

Wooded cliff

BLAKEMERE

Monnington Falls
grade 2-3

MONNINGTON
-ON-WYE

TYBERTON

PRESTON-
ON-WYE

•233
Garnons Hill

shallows

MADLEY

R. Wye.

BRIDGE SOLLERS

A438

The Weir Gardens

B-4399

THE WEIR

RUCKHALL COMMON

Island, shoot left

Eaton Camp

| 0 m. | | 1 | | 2 |
| 0 km. | 1 | | 2 | 3 |

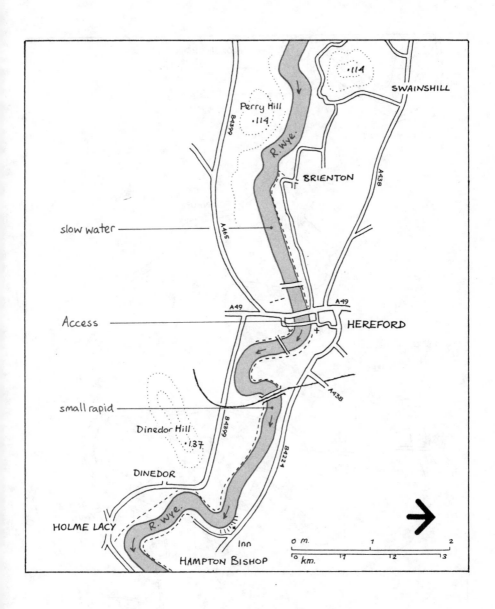

slow water

Access

small rapid

SWAINSHILL

·114

Perry Hill
·114.

R. Wye.

BRIENTON

B4399

A438

A465

A49

A49

HEREFORD

A438

Dinedor Hill
·137.

B4399

B4224

DINEDOR

R. Wye.

HOLME LACY

Inn

HAMPTON BISHOP

0 m.   1   2
0 km.   1   2   3

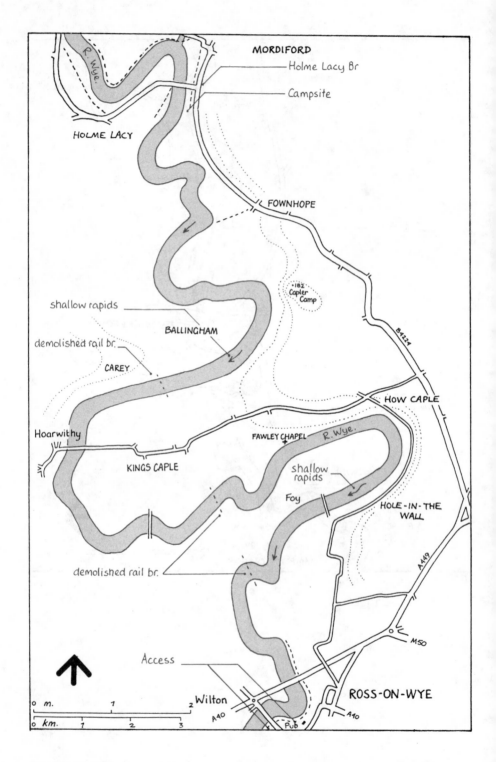

MORDIFORD

Holme Lacy Br

Campsite

HOLME LACY

R. Wye

FOWNHOPE

·182
Capler
Camp

shallow rapids

BALLINGHAM

demolished rail br.

CAREY

B4224

How CAPLE

Hoarwithy

FAWLEY CHAPEL

R. Wye.

KINGS CAPLE

shallow
rapids

Foy

HOLE-IN-THE
WALL

demolished rail br.

A449

M50

Access

Wilton

ROSS-ON-WYE

A40

A40

Pub

o   m.   1   2

o   km.   1   2   3

Hereford to Ross-on-Wye

Start (509396)   Finish (596244)   Grade 1   Distance 29mls/48km (Hereford to Holme Lacy 9mls/15km Holme Lacy to Hoarwithy 9mls/15km   Hoarwithy to Court Farm/Hole-in-the-Wall 6mls/10km Hole-in-the-Wall to Ross-on-Wye 5mls/8km)

At Hereford access is on the right just beyond the old bridge. The cathedral is on the left and a little way further is the Victorian suspension bridge. A mile further on, the river passes under a railway bridge, and you are now out of the town. The steep banks of the river almost obscure the views over the surrounding floodplain pastures – there is a line of hills ahead, towards which the river flows. At Hampton Bishop a high flood bank almost hides the Bunch of Carrots public house behind it. This slow stretch of river is a favourite fishing spot for anglers as there are many still pools.

Four miles beyond Hampton Bishop the River Lugg enters the Wye on the left. Nearby is the village of Mordiford, famed for its legend of a dragon who preyed on local sheep and shepherds. It was eventually slain by a condemned criminal seeking a pardon for his crimes. Unfortunately he was incinerated by the dragon's dying breath.

Half a mile further on is Holme Lacy Bridge and a campsite on the left just downstream. There are occasional small rapids as the river meanders towards Capler Hill and here the wooded hillsides run down to the river edge. High above is Capler Camp, an ancient earthwork and the remains of a Roman camp. The river bends right into a long stretch with the odd island and shallow rapid. There are steeply wooded banks on the left and the remains of the first of three demolished Great Western Railway bridges that you will pass on the way to Ross.

The large loop in the river leads to Hoarwithy Bridge and village at the western end. Access is on the left below the bridge. The river then doubles back to How Caple, passing a footbridge at Sellack, the second demolished railway bridge and Fawley chapel on the left bank. Again wooded hills come down to the river on the left. Court Farm is passed on the left. This is main canoeing centre for PGL activity holidays. Here there are small rapids leading down to Foy footbridge.

Beyond Foy the third demolished railway bridge is reached after more shallow rapids and from here it's just over a couple of miles to Ross. Before you reach the town you will probably see the steeple of Ross church which is perched on a high bluff over the river. A convenient stopping point is the Hope and Anchor public house on the left below the town. A further half-mile brings you to Wilton Bridge, where there is good access on the left just beyond the bridge.

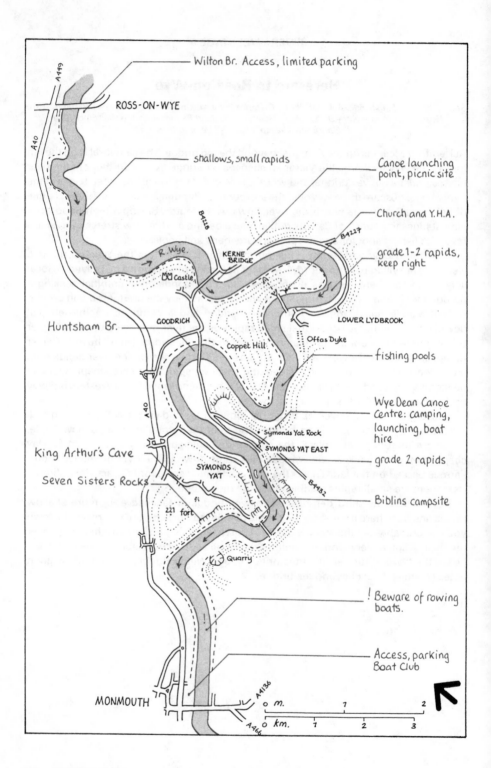

Wilton Br. Access, limited parking

ROSS-ON-WYE

A449

A40

shallows, small rapids

Canoe launching point, picnic site

Church and Y.H.A.

B4228

R. Wye.

KERNE BRIDGE

Castle

B4227

grade 1-2 rapids, keep right

LOWER LYDBROOK

Huntsham Br.

GOODRICH

Coppet Hill

Offas Dyke

fishing pools

A40

Symonds Yat Rock

Wye Dean Canoe Centre: camping, launching, boat hire

SYMONDS YAT EAST

grade 2 rapids

King Arthur's Cave

Seven Sisters Rocks

SYMONDS YAT

B4432

Biblins campsite

221 fort

Quarry

! Beware of rowing boats.

Access, parking Boat Club

MONMOUTH

A4136

0 m. 7 2

A466

0 km. 1 2 3

Ross-on-Wye to Monmouth

Start (596244)   Finish (512128)   Grade 1 – 2   Distance 21mls/35km (Ross-on-Wye to Kerne Bridge 6mls/10km   Kerne Bridge to Symonds Yat 9mls/15km   Symonds Yat to Monmouth 6mls/10km)

This is perhaps the most popular canoeing stretch on the lower Wye and one of the most popular in Britain. The rapids at the picturesque resort of Symonds Yat attract countless canoeists throughout the year and provide an introduction to whitewater for beginners and novices, being an excellent training ground for moving water skills and slalom practice. At Symonds Yat the Wye Dean Canoe Centre offers boat hire and instruction and mountain bike hire for those who want to explore the countless trails of the Forest of Dean.

From Wilton Bridge at Ross it is easy going through pleasant scenery with the odd shallow rapid. After about three miles Goodrich Castle can be seen towering impressively above the river. It is possible to walk up to the castle from the right bank but landing is awkward because of the short steep muddy banks. Kerne Bridge is passed shortly beyond this. There is a canoe launching point just below Kerne Bridge on the left.

A long stretch of river with wooded banks on the right and the occasional house on the left takes you round to Lydbrook. There is a pub on the left bank and shallow rocky rapids below, best taken to the right. There is a church and youth hostel on the right at Welsh Bickner and, just beyond, a disused railway bridge crosses the river. Ahead there are tall cliffs, the largest being Yat Rock – a popular tourist look-out. This part of the river is also a fishing area and there are notices asking you to pass through the fishing pools without stopping.

The valley sides open out as the river begins a loop, passing under Huntsham Bridge, through another fishing area and around to Symonds Yat West with hotels on the right. There is a large rock by the left-hand bank near here which is often used for seal launching.

A little further down is Symonds Yat East and the concrete steps of the Wye Dean Canoe Centre and Campsite, with tea shops and a pub beyond. Beware of the pleasure cruisers that motor up and down this part of the river. A couple of hundred yards downstream the river changes from its gentle pace as it rushes into a long Grade 2 rapid around an island. This is the popular Symonds Yat rapid and on busy weekends it can get very crowded.

The scenery below Symonds Yat is impressive, with steeply forested valley sides and rocky outcrops and all around the shrill cries of birdlife. For a moment you could be mistaken for thinking you were on a river in South America. Biblins Forestry Commission campsite is on the right by a suspended footbridge and beyond that there are pathways up to the rocky outcrops of Seven Sisters Rocks for fine views over the river. Behind Seven Sisters' Rocks is King Arthur's Cave, once a home for the early caveman. Another four miles from Biblins brings you out of the 'jungle' and onto a long stretch of slow water to Monmouth, where it is important to keep alert as the section is frequented by a very active rowing club. Finish at the Boat Club by the concrete steps on the right just above the bridge.

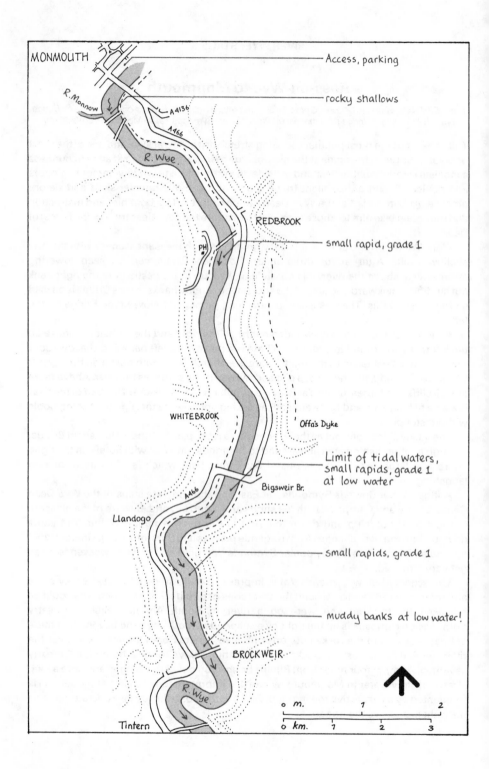

MONMOUTH

R. Monnow

A 4136

A 466

R. Wye

REDBROOK

PH

WHITEBROOK

Offa's Dyke

A 466

Bigsweir Br.

Llandogo

BROCKWEIR

R. Wye

Tintern

Access, parking

rocky shallows

small rapid, grade 1

Limit of tidal waters, small rapids, grade 1 at low water

small rapids, grade 1

muddy banks at low water!

o m.   1   2

o km.   1   2   3

Monmouth to Chepstow

Start (512128)   Finish (535944)   Grade 1 – 2   Distance 20mls/32km (Monmouth to Bigsweir 6mls/10km   Bigsweir to Tintern 7mls/11km   Tintern to Chepstow 7mls/11km)

Just after Monmouth Bridge the River Monnow joins the Wye on the right. There are small rapids caused by underwater obstructions from the debris of the demolished railway bridges. The river now flows through a wooded valley with fields on either side. At Redbrook there are some large boulders in the river and a shallow rapid after the disused railway bridge. There is an excellent pub on the right which is well worth checking out, always mindful of the 'don't canoe and drink alcohol' dictum in the river safety section of this book!

At Bigsweir the main road crosses the river and this point marks the general limit of the tidal water as the river approaches the Severn Estuary. There is a small rapid below the bridge. One mile further on the village of Llandogo is situated next to the river on the right bank.

There are occasional small rapids between Llandogo and Tintern but it can be smooth at high water. The banks are now muddy and it is difficult to exit from the river without getting messy, especially at Brockweir, three miles further on. If you do decide on a mud fight be warned that it can take several showers to remove the slime. The remains of wharfs and quays here are a reminder that this was once a major boat-building port on the lower Wye. It was here that the sailing boats unloaded their goods into barges which were then pulled by teams of men up to Monmouth, Ross and Hereford and even as far as Hay.

At Tintern it is possible to land on the right below the bridge and next to the car-park at the Abbey. This is a popular tourist site in the spring and summer and parking may be difficult.

The twelfth century Cistercian Abbey is a prominent landmark and well worth a visit. The remaining stretch of river from Tintern to Chepstow is broad and flat except at low water when awkward rapids, the remains of old weirs, are exposed. For this reason, and to make best use of the tides, canoeists are advised to leave Tintern not later than one hour after high water and travel straight through to Chepstow. (High water at Tintern is four hours before high water at Dover.) It is difficult, if not impossible, to land on this stretch, owing to the mud banks; however, this shouldn't deter you for the river flows through an impressive valley with high rocky outcrops above steeply wooded sides and tall vertical cliffs dropping straight down to the water. At Chepstow the castle is situated on top of a high cliff on the right, making a dramatic end to the river journey. The best finishing point is on the right bank at the public slipway below the first bridge. Beyond this the A48 and the railway cross the river and the Wye continues to the Severn Estuary. It is not advisable to go beyond Chepstow because of dangerous currents.

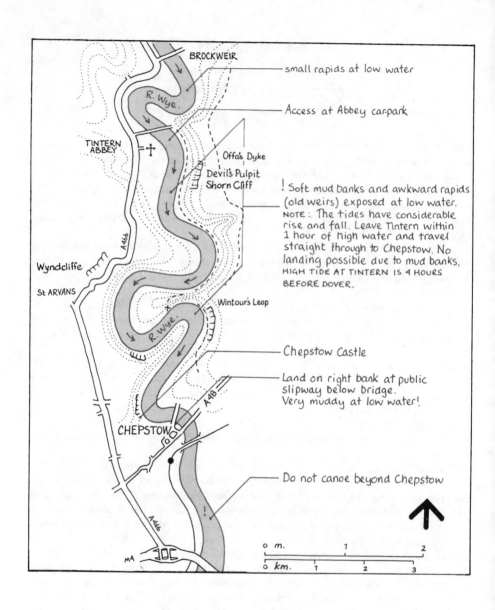

BROCKWEIR

small rapids at low water

R. Wye.

Access at Abbey carpark

TINTERN
ABBEY

Offa's Dyke

Devil's Pulpit
Shorn Cliff

! Soft mud banks and awkward rapids (old weirs) exposed at low water. NOTE: The tides have considerable rise and fall. Leave Tintern within 1 hour of high water and travel straight through to Chepstow. No landing possible due to mud banks. HIGH TIDE AT TINTERN IS 4 HOURS BEFORE DOVER.

Wyndcliffe

St ARVANS

Wintour's Leap

R. Wye.

Chepstow Castle

Land on right bank at public slipway below bridge. Very muddy at low water!

CHEPSTOW

Do not canoe beyond Chepstow

0 m.   1   2
0 km.   1   2   3

RIVER USK

SENNYBRIDGE TO CRICKHOWELL

OS Sheets 160/161   27 miles/43km   Grade 2 – 3

The River Usk has its source in the northern foothills of the Black Mountains towards the western end of the Brecon Beacons National Park – and is fed by the numerous streams that flow down from these mountains. The river cuts an easterly course past Brecon and then to Abergavenny before turning southwards to Newport and into the Severn Estuary. Its proximity to the River Wye makes it easy to combine venues although there is enough canoeing at various grades to keep any group of paddlers happy for a weekend. Over the years the Usk has become a popular river for those people wishing to undertake an easy to moderate whitewater river descents and sections of the river are also used for canoeing competitions. The main section described, Sennybridge to Crickhowell, is noted for its many rapids set in fine scenery with deep valleys, open fields and with mountain views all around. Below Crickhowell the river calms and its gentler pace would be ideal for canoe tours through Abergavenny to the old market town of Usk.

Access considerations on the River Usk

There is an access agreement for the Usk which has been operating successfully for a number of years without problems. Permission is required for canoeing through the Glanusk Estate as it can conflict with gun sports. Full details of agreements, access points, addresses and local information are obtainable from the Access Officer (WCA).

Note: For general location map of the River Usk see page 125.

Sennybridge to Brecon

Start (920236)   Finish (037289)   Grade 3   Distance 9mls/14km

To the west of Brecon the A40 passes through Sennybridge. A little further west take the turn signposted Sennybridge Camp and just before the camp gates turn right. Put in at the corner of the road near the river. Be considerate to the occupier of the adjacent house and his lawn and do not block the road with cars. There are small rapids and occasional shallows as the river flows through lightly wooded banks.

Shortly after the first road bridge there are three falls where the river drops over horizontal bedrock. The first is on a right-hand bend and in low water take the channel around to the right of an island above and descend a right-hand shoot over the sill. In high water it would be wise to inspect this drop for any trees and for alternative routes along the width of the fall. The second fall is shortly afterwards and is a little higher, usually run on the left on low water but again, in higher flows, inspection will be necessary to check the strength of the stopper and to choose alternative routes. Some bouldery rapids lead down to the third – somewhat dangerous – fall, which is marked by a small cliff on the left. Inspect from the left and shoot middle to right in medium to high water as a vicious stopper can occur on the left. In low water it can be run in one drop on the left. These three falls can be easily portaged if necessary.

After the Sennybridge Falls the river flows through woodland with occasional steep banks, all of which add to the beauty of this run. There are plenty of small Grade 2 – 3 rapids to entertain you as you make your way down towards Brecon, past Abercamlais and Penpont bridges, under the stone arches of Aberbran Bridge, and finally through a steeply forested valley before the long flat stretch to the boat club and car-park just before Brecon. This is an ideal take-out point as just downstream is a weir which can be a shallow scrape in low water, though it can be portaged.

Another alternative exit point for a shorter run during short days or low water is at Aberbran, on the left above the bridge. However, seek permission first at Aberbran Fach Farm. No access should be used at the private bridges of Abercamlais and Penpont.

Brecon to Talybont

Start (037289)   Finish (122233)   Grade 1 – 2 plus two weirs   Distance 7mls/12km

This is an ideal trip for the novice paddler or for those who just like to take things easy, drifting and paddling along quiet waters with views of rounded, tree-clad hills and distant mountains. From Brecon Weir (038289) the river is gentle for the first few miles posing no problems to the canoeist. It passes under the A40 and then under the B4558 and the Brynich aqueduct that carries the Monmouthshire and Brecon Canal.

Just below the aqueduct there are Grade 1 rapids as the river curves gently around to the right. Up on the left is a farm and a short distance beyond this old mill buildings are passed. Be cautious here as there is a small but rocky weir (084269) which can be

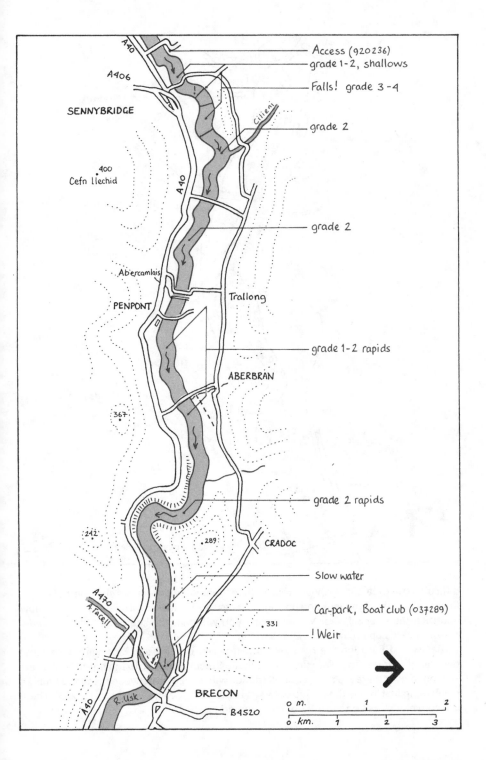

Access (920236)
grade 1-2, shallows
Falls! grade 3-4

grade 2

grade 2

grade 1-2 rapids

grade 2 rapids

Slow water

Car-park, Boat club (037289)
! Weir

A40
A406
SENNYBRIDGE
Cilieni
A40
400
Cefn llechid
Abercamlais
PENPONT
Trallong
ABERBRAN
367
242
289
CRADOC
A470
A Face!!
331
A40
R. Usk.
BRECON
B4520

o m.   1   2
o km.   1   2   3

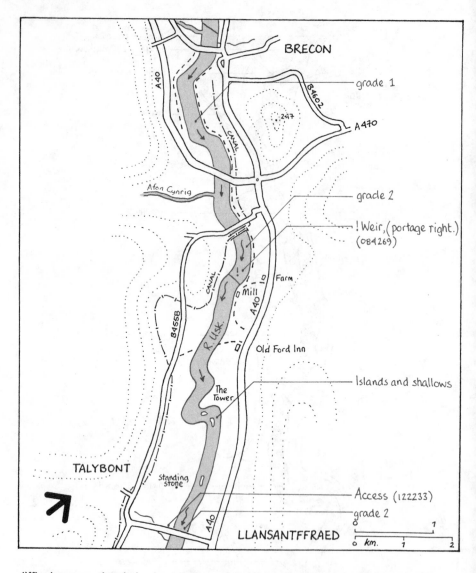

grade 1

grade 2

! Weir, (portage right.)
(084269)

Islands and shallows

Access (122233)

grade 2

BRECON

A470

Afon Cynrig

Farm

Mill

Old Ford Inn

The Tower

TALYBONT

Standing stone

LLANSANTFFRAED

R. USK

CANAL

difficult to negotiate in low water, through in higher flows there is a shoot left of centre (inspect from the right bank and portage if necessary). A few small shallow rapids follow and then the river relaxes. Not far below you will pass the site of an old ford, and a hundred yards up on the left is Old Ford Inn.

Below Old Ford Inn the river banks flatten out into grazing land with occasional overhanging trees. There are fine views of the Brecon Beacons to the right. On this last section of river there are several small islands with shallows between them and finally a small rapid just above the bridge between Llansantffraed and Talybont (122233). There is a convenient exit on the right before the bridge.

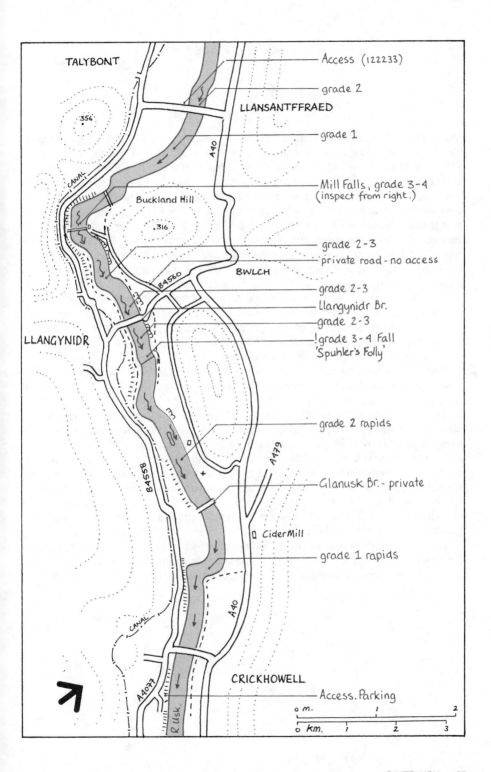

TALYBONT

Access (122233)

grade 2

LLANSANTFFRAED

grade 1

.356

CANAL

A40

Mill Falls, grade 3-4
(inspect from right.)

Buckland Hill

.316

grade 2-3

private road - no access

B4560

BWLCH

grade 2-3

Llangynidr Br.

grade 2-3

!grade 3-4 Fall
'Spuhler's Folly'

LLANGYNIDR

grade 2 rapids

A479

B4558

Glanusk Br.- private

Cider Mill

grade 1 rapids

CANAL

A40

A4077

CRICKHOWELL

Access. Parking

R. Usk.

o m.   1   2

o km.   1   2   3

Talybont to Crickhowell

Start (122233)   Finish (220176)   Grade 3   Distance 12mls/19km

Many groups that come to the Usk for a weekend usually run the Sennybridge to Brecon stretch one day and the Talybont to Crickhowell section the next, missing out Stage 2. From the A40 take the Talybont turn-off and cross over the bridge. There is a stile here and canoes and kayaks can be launched at the aforementioned exit point upstream of the bridge on the right bank. There is limited parking so do not obstruct the road, larger vehicles are best left at the lay-by and toilets on the A40 towards Crickhowell. From the bridge there are the occasional Grade 1 rapids as the river flows around Buckland Hill towards Mill Falls. The approach to Mill Falls is heralded by the gauging building on the right bank, Llaiddelty Church, also on the right, and by iron gates on the left bank.

At the start of Mill Falls the first drop, through a broken weir, is usually run on the right down a fast shoot with calmer water below and a large breakout on the right. The next rapid below can be a tricky Grade 3, best taken on the left towards the Mill buildings. The right-hand drops can be run but beware of bottoming out (inspection or portage should be carried out on the right bank if necessary). There are plenty of small playspots here and on the rapids below but please avoid upsetting the occupiers of the Mill buildings as you are in their front garden!

Below the Mill the steep banks and rocky outcrops give an air of seclusion to the next stretch of the river. There are more Grade 2 – 3 rapids and a series of islands, with a final long rapid leading down to Llangynidr Bridge.

The rapids below Llangynidr Bridge should be treated with caution for in medium to high flows there is a powerful stopper where the river drops over bedrock. Further down, where the river takes a left-hand bend with a rocky outcrop on the right, there is a fall across the river known as 'Spuhlers Folly'. It can be easily inspected from the left bank and is usually run on a left-hand route through a slot and boils or in low flows over the centre. But beware, for in high flows there is a dangerous stopper across the right.

Below Spuhlers Folly there are several Grade 2 rapids, another island to pass and a church on the left before the Glanusk Estate bridge, with its gate tower, is reached. From here to Crickhowell the river is wide and slow with the occasional Grade 1 rapid.

At Crickhowell it is best to continue on under the bridge for another half-mile to a point where there is a lay-by on the right above a steep bank. As there is ample room to park cars it is preferable to finish here to avoid obstructing roads and crossing fences at Crickhowell.

12 River Marteg (Wye tributary) – at the main falls

13   *River Usk – shooting Mill Falls*

14   *River Wye – at Symonds Yat*

15 *River Dee – Llangollen Town Falls*

17 River Dee – Town Falls in spate conditions

16 Afon Tryweryn – the Fedwr-gog Falls

19 20 *Afon Conwy – views of the Fairy Glen*

21 Afon Conwy – the first big rapid below Conwy Falls

AFON TRYWERYN

LLYN CELYN DAM TO BALA

OS Sheet 125   5 miles/8km   Grade 3 – 4

The Tryweryn is unique amongst the rivers included in this guide in that its water flow is controlled by releases from the Llyn Celyn Dam. Just because it's raining it doesn't mean that the dam will be releasing as there may be enough water already in the River Dee, into which the Tryweryn flows just below Lake Bala, and any more could cause flooding. Alternatively, if it hasn't rained for some time there is a good chance of releases; for this reason the river is often a prime venue during the summer for clubs and individuals using it as a training ground for slalom, river racing and whitewater skills, and it can provide endless fun and exhilaration for novice and expert alike.

The Tryweryn also has the added status of being a National Whitewater Centre where competitions are held and training courses are undertaken. In 1981 the river gained international status by hosting the World Slalom and River Racing Championships; since then its development has seen improved pathways, car-parks, changing rooms and toilets. A charge is levied for use of the facilities and the river, which contributes to the running costs of the Centre.

The Tryweryn's proximity to Llangollen and North Wales makes it an ideal alternative venue when other rivers are too low to paddle, though it is best to telephone the Centre in advance to check on its availability and whether there are any competitions or organised tours taking place.

The Whitewater Centre (892402), Canolfan Tryweryn, is reached from a turning off the A4212 near Ciltagarth (892401) between Bala and Llyn Celyn. There is camping available nearby.

Access considerations on the River Tryweryn

The River Tryweryn is dam-controlled. Information on releases for the slalom site and for access to the river is obtainable from the National Whitewater Centre. Access is controlled for both summer and winter use by the Canoeing Management Officer who is responsible for the maintenance and upkeep of the river. A fee is payable for use. A telephone answering machine (☎ 0678 520826) is in operation to advise of water levels and availability.

Note: For general location map of Afon Tryweryn see page 112.

Llyn Celyn Dam to Tyn-y-cornel Bridge (slalom site)

Start (881398)   Finish (896400)   Grade 3 – 4   Distance 1½mls/2km

This section is open for public use when the dam is releasing and provided that there are no scheduled competitions taking place. A phone call in advance will confirm availability and the level of water release from the dam. The concentration of Grade 3 – 4 rapids and falls here provide endless possibilities for training and playing. There are pathways along the banks enabling you to inspect all sections and to choose where to start from depending on your ability and enthusiasm. If you are going to start up near the dam check in at the Centre first to collect your bib and pay your fee. If you arrive early enough or have camped by the river then take a walk along this section to view it in low water conditions before the dam water is released. When the water is 'turned-on' it takes just a few minutes for the Tryweryn to turn from an insignificant trickle to a raging torrent.

From below the dam a weir drops into the stilling pool and beyond that there are small fast rapids leading down to a small weir just above the Irish Bridge. Below the bridge a flat section takes you down to the fish pass, a large metal sieve across the river. The section above the fish pass is only available to organised courses as the Irish Bridge has dangerous siphons on the right-hand side. Public use and rafting begins below the fish pass.

Around a left-hand corner 'The Graveyard' begins, a long Grade 3 – 4 rapid. In high flows there can be excellent play holes on this section; however, the rapid is not named like this for nothing. It is fast and technical, requiring skill and awareness to avoid broaching on rocks or capsizing. There is a brief respite before the river channels to the left down a fast shoot with a 'grippy' stopper at the bottom.

Another long fast shoot follows before the Fedwr-gog Falls under the first bridge. This is usually run to the right. More small rapids follow on towards the 'Dog-Leg' where there is a small stopper and waves to play on and a large eddy on the right. The next large rapid is just above 'Scaffold Bridge', with another favourite playspot on the final wave. Then there are fifty yards of calm before Chapel Falls, a steep drop with a stopper that ensnares many canoeists. However there is a pool below in which those despatched from their boats can recover.

From Chapel Falls to Tyn-y-cornel Bridge is an ideal section of Grade 2 rapids suitable for those beginning whitewater canoeing. It is very convenient as an exit by the rock ramp on the right above the bridge allows an easy carry back as far as you want for another run.

Tyn-y-cornel Bridge to Bala (A494 bridge)

Start (895399)   Finish (929362)   Grade 2 – 3 (Mill Falls, 4)   Distance 4mls/6km

Many people who come to the Tryweryn tend to concentrate their efforts on the top section. However, if you have the chance and the lower river is open for canoeing, then

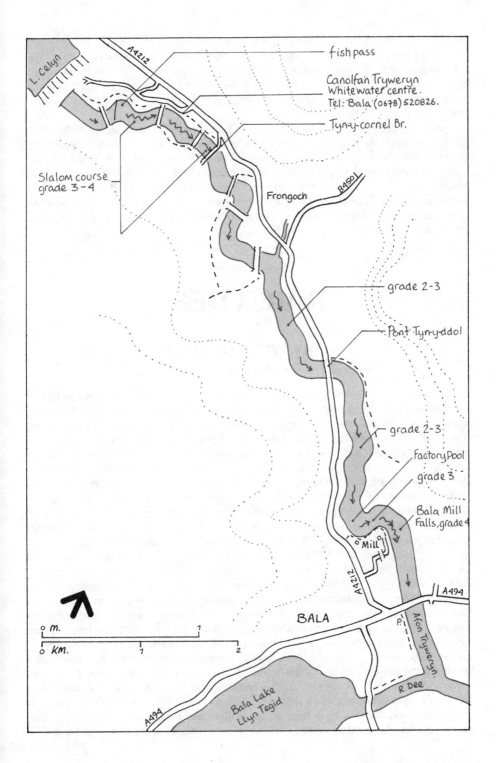

L. Celyn

A4212

fish pass

Canolfan Tryweryn
Whitewater centre.
Tel: Bala (0678) 520826.

Tyn-y-cornel Br.

Slalom course
grade 3-4

Frongoch

B4501

grade 2-3

Pont Tyn-y-ddol

grade 2-3

Factory Pool

grade 3

Bala Mill
Falls, grade 4

Mill

A4212

A494

BALA

P.

Afon Tryweryn

R Dee

o m.   1

o KM.   1   2

Bala Lake
Llyn Tegid

A494

the four-mile run down to Bala Mill is well worth doing. On this section there are frequent Grade 2 – 3 rapids between wooded banks yet with open views of the surrounding hills. The river passes under the A4212 at Pont Tyn y ddol and continues on towards Bala Mill Falls. You can exit before the falls at Factory Pool (920367) where a path leads up to the road on the right. However, if you have got this far, then it is worth continuing on to challenge the Mill Falls.

From the Factory Pool there are further rapids (Grade 3) on the approach to Bala Mill Falls (Grade 4). River racers tend to opt for a 'chicken-shoot' on the left to save time but the main fall on the right can be negotiated without too many problems. These falls are easy to inspect from the right-hand bank. After the Bala Mill Falls, continue to the A494 road bridge and exit on the right bank next to the car-park. Below this the river flows into the Afon Dyfrwdy, better known as the River Dee. To the west, Lake Bala is another prime watersports location for sailing and windsurfing, and during the summer months the campsites and town can be very busy.

RIVER DEE

CORWEN TO OVERTON

OS Sheets 117/125   32 miles/51km   Grade 2 – 4

Shared between Wales and England, the River Dee is canoeable for its entire length from its outflow at Lake Bala (Llyn Tegid) and the confluence of the River Tryweryn down to Chester. The most popular stretch of the river for canoeists begins fifteen miles from Bala where the wide 'valley of the Dee', known in welsh as 'Glyndyfrdwy' turns eastward at Corwen and begins to narrow down as it approaches the Horseshoe Pass and the Vale of Llangollen. Hemmed in by a steep-sided valley with the Berwyn Mountains to the south, the River Dee provides excellent scenic runs with easy rapids from Corwen to Overton. There are however two miles of turbulence between the Horseshoe Falls and Llangollen, where there are many large rapids.

If you wish to avoid the whitewater at Horseshoe Falls it is an easy matter to transfer your canoe to the feeder channel of the Shropshire Union Canal and to take an easy and gentle by-pass down to Llangollen. This short, turbulent section of river, which was once deemed 'unsuitable for canoes', has become one of the most popular canoeing venues in Britain. Llangollen has hosted numerous national and international slalom and river racing competitions on the rapids of the Dee, but it is perhaps more favoured for the large canoe tours and rallies that are organised on the river each year. These are the best times to paddle the river and although it can get crowded there is always an atmosphere of good fellowship. The most notable of these events is the annual *Mike Jones Rally*, run as a tribute to a canoeist whose exploits and films inspired many to take up the sport but who tragically lost his life whilst rescuing a colleague on the Braldu River in Pakistan in 1978. Up to two thousand canoeists have been known to attend this weekend event which ensures a welcome boost to the winter economy of the town.

Below Llangollen the river regains its gentler pace except for a Grade 3 rapid at Trevor Rocks which was the venue for the first canoe slalom competition held in Britain

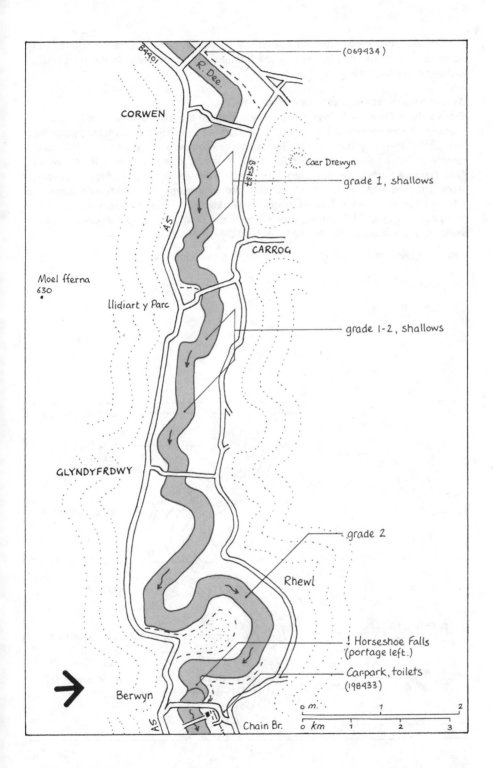

(069434)

CORWEN

B4401

R. Dee.

B5437

Caer Drewyn

grade 1, shallows

A5

CARROG

Moel fferna
630

Llidiart y Parc

grade 1-2, shallows

GLYNDYFRDWY

grade 2

Rhewl

! Horseshoe Falls
(portage left.)

Car-park, toilets
(198433)

Berwyn

A5

Chain Br.

0 m.   1   2

0 km   1   2   3

in 1939. Beyond Overton the hills fall away to the flat plain of Chester and the river becomes slow and lethargic as it meanders in tight bends towards the tidal weir at Chester more than thirty miles away.

Access considerations on the River Dee
From Bala to Corwen the river runs slow and there are parts where wire is stretched across it to keep livestock from wandering. Corwen provides a good access point for a tour of the most popular section. Gaining access can be a lengthy process due to the large number of riparian owners involved. There is an agreement from Corwen to Glyndyfrdwy during the close season providing notice of a trip is given in advance. Access to the Llangollen stretch is restricted to a number of weekends agreed in advance between the Dee Users Committee and Llangollen anglers to cover touring and competition events. A list of riparian owners and details of all agreements and open weekends is available from the Local Access Officer (WCA).

Note: For general location map of the River Dee see page 112.

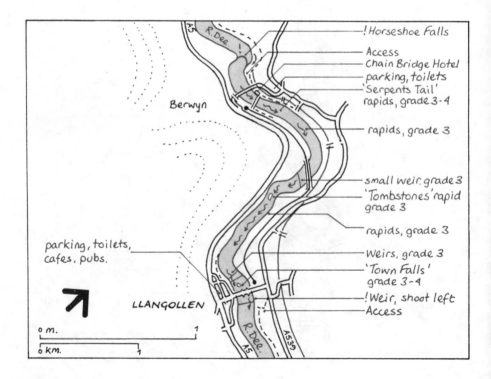

Corwen to Horseshoe Falls

Start (069434)   Finish (196433)   Grade 2   Distance 12mls/20km

This section of the river, first running through fields with flanking hills and then entering an ever deepening valley, is attractive yet uncomplicated with the occasional small rapid. Because of this it has become a popular run for canoe tourers and novice whitewater paddlers. At Corwen the river has already travelled fifteen miles from Lake Bala and for much of this distance it is broad and flat. From Corwen, where the A5 crosses the river (069434), to Carrog the river is gentle and slow moving.

Access at Corwen is on the left, just downstream of the A5 bridge. The river has now altered its course eastward and the scenery becomes more inspiring with steep valley sides and tree-lined banks.

Carrog is an alternative starting point (115436) where it is possible to put in on the right bank above the bridge. From Carrog to the Horseshoe Falls, a distance of eight miles, there are small rapids up to Grade 2 with calmer sections between in which to idle at the pace of the river. The rapids can be long and rocky in low water or fast and bouncy with many small playspots in higher flows. Some of the shallow rapids on this section will be washed out in high water.

Glyndyfrdwy Bridge marks the half-way point on this stretch of river. Before Horseshoe Falls is reached the river takes in a large loop. Rhewl is on the left and the road is close to the left bank. There are further Grade 2 rapids leading down to the falls.

Horseshoe Falls is a dangerous weir (196433) and an exit should be made on the left bank. It can be run around to the left down a rocky broken drop (Grade 3) but avoid the centre which has been the site of many mishaps and near drownings in the past. The weir pool feeds the Shropshire Union Canal and if you are finishing here you can either walk along the towpath, past the Chain Bridge Hotel, and up the metal staircase to the car-park above or paddle the next hundred yards along the canal. If you want to miss out the next two miles of Grade 3 – 4 rapids then carry on down the canal towards Llangollen.

Horseshoe Falls to Llangollen

Start (196433)   Finish (217421)   Grade 3 – 4   Distance 2mls/3km

From the car-park above the Chain Bridge (196433) a metal staircase crosses the canal and leads down to the Chain Bridge Hotel. Carry your canoes the two hundred yards up the towpath to put in just below the Horseshoe Falls Weir. The next two miles of river are packed with numerous rapids and notable playspots and it is easy to understand why this has become one of the best-known and most popular whitewater runs in the country. Although the section is Graded 3 – 4 it is an ideal stretch for aspiring whitewater canoeists to test their skills, for rescue is easy in the calm sections below each rapid and with proper care and awareness there should be no injuries or mishaps.

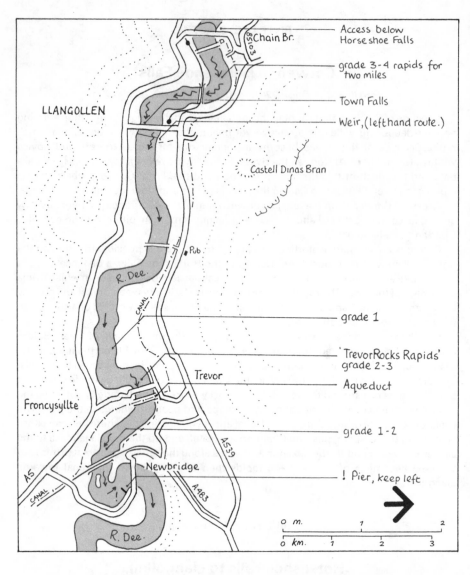

Access below
Horse shoe Falls

grade 3-4 rapids for
two miles

Town Falls

Weir, (lefthand route.)

Chain Br.

LLANGOLLEN

Castell Dinas Bran

Pub

R. Dee.

CANAL

grade 1

'TrevorRocks Rapids'
grade 2-3

Trevor

Aqueduct

Froncysyllte

grade 1-2

Newbridge

! Pier, keep left

A5

CANAL

A539

A483

R. Dee.

o m.   1   2
o km.   1   2   3

From the put-in the river flows swiftly under the road bridge and into a Grade 2 – 3
rapid under the Chain Bridge; 200 hundred yards below lies the 'Serpent's Tail'. At the
Serpent's Tail the river is forced into a narrow channel between a rock face on the right
and flat bedrock on the left. In low water this is a boily chute with a series of standing
waves at the beginning. In medium water there are turbulent breakouts half-way down
and a powerful stopper at the final constrictions. The exposed bedrock on the left
provides an ideal spot for watching the excitement of the canoeists descending this
rapid. In high flows the bedrock is covered and a large stopper forms on the right ready
to catch the unwary. Below, the river twists through an 'S' bend of boily water before a
calm run down to the next rapid.

The next whitewater stretch is at a broken weir with a fast breakout to the left and surfacing waves below. Beyond the railway bridge is Halfway Weir, usually run to the left and around the next left-hand bend lies 'The Tombstones'. There used to be two concrete stanchions in midstream at the top of this broken weir, upon which the unwitting somehow found themselves trapped. These have now been removed to make the rapid safer and the best route is around to the far left. Immediately below lies a small stopper ideal for practice and play.

After the Tombstones the next left-hand bend leads into another Grade 3 rapid with more play waves – a section (next to the old mill on the right) often used for slalom training and competitions.

The lead up to the Town Falls begins a short distance beyond the old mill. The bridge can be seen in the distance and if you are unsure of your route here then it is best to head off to the right bank to land and inspect. A small weir, run on a central spout leads to 'The Pot', a corkscrewing chute on the right of the river which leads into the Town Falls. The best route on the Town Falls can be checked when you first arrive in Llangollen as the water-level often dictates your choice. In higher flows you can run the river on the left. Llangollen Bridge is a favourite spectating spot and a capsize will guarantee a loud cheer from the audience. If someone does capsize here then make sure they are rescued quickly as there is a weir just a short way down stream. This has a nasty drop on the right but a clear chute to the left. Finish just below this weir on the left and carry up to the road. If your car is at the Chain Bridge then it is convenient to carry your boat up to the canal behind the Bridge End Pub and paddle back 'up river'.

Llangollen to Overton Bridge

Start (217421)   Finish (355427)   Grade 2 (2 – 3 rapid at Trevor)   Distance 17½mls/28km

Below Llangollen the river is broad and swift with overhanging trees on the banks constituting the main hazard. It flows through the Vale of Llangollen, past pleasant flood plain pastures backed by steep-sided wooded hills. Above Llangollen are the ruins of Castell Dinas Bran, situated on a prominent hill that rises to just over 1000ft and whence superb views of the Dee can be gained. A rocky escarpment runs behind the ruins. One and a half miles from Llangollen a footbridge crosses the river (239422). From here a track leads up to the canal and the Sun Trevor Hotel.

Below the footbridge the valley narrows and just above a medieval stone bridge lies 'Trevor Rocks Rapid' (268421). This is Grade 2 – 3 and can provide plenty of standing waves to play on in medium to high river levels. A road runs on the left, upstream of the bridge and close to the river just above the rapids.

Beyond the road bridge are the towering spans of Pont Cysyllte Aqueduct. This 1007ft-long structure, rising over 120ft above the river, was designed by Thomas Telford, who also designed the Horseshoe Falls Weir. It was eventually opened in 1805 after ten years of work. Small shallow rapids run below and around the next bend in the river. Before Newbridge is reached a railway viaduct crosses the river. There is a concrete pier built out into the river just before Newbridge on the right-hand side.

Below Newbridge the river enters a deep wooded valley with Halton Woods on the right. This then broadens out into fields and woods with the occasional small rapid or

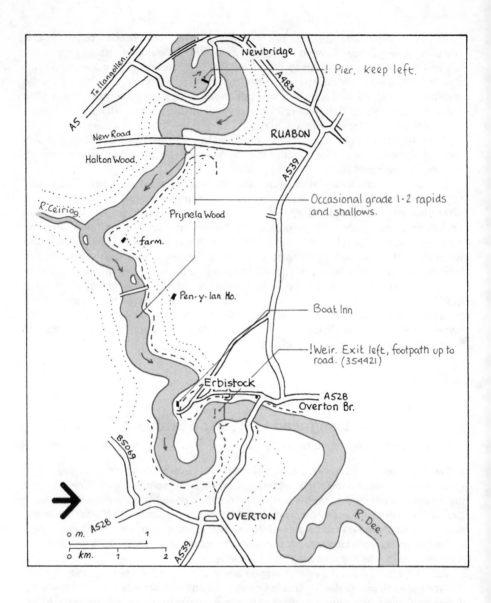

Newbridge

! Pier, keep left.

To llangollen

A5

A483

New Road

RUABON

Halton Wood.

A539

R. Ceiriog.

Prynela Wood

Occasional grade 1-2 rapids and shallows.

farm.

Pen-y-lan Ho.

Boat Inn

!Weir. Exit left, footpath up to road. (354421)

Erbistock

A528
Overton Br.

B5069

OVERTON

R. Dee.

o m. A528   1

o km.   1   2

A539

shallows and a few islands. The Afon Ceiriog enters from the right below Halton Woods and from here it is another four miles to Erbistock (356413). There is a footbridge that crosses the river just below Pen-y-lan House.

At Erbistock there is a sixteenth century inn and restaurant and a church on the left bank. There is one large final meander left before the river breaks out into the flat plain of Chester at Overton Bridge (355427). Just upstream of the bridge is a weir, on a sharp right-hand bend, with a mill building on the left. Exit on the left above the weir where there is a footpath up to the road to finish this scenic canoe tour.

AFON CONWY

YSBYTY IFAN TO BETWS-Y-COED

OS Sheet 116   9 miles/14km   Grade 3 – 5

The Afon Conwy is a river of contrasts. In its lower reaches it is broad and calm, but in its upper reaches, having gained its volume and power from the many streams that drain a high peaty moorland, it descends powerfully through numerous deep gorges. Its extensive catchment area ensures that there is usually enough water in the Conwy long after the other rivers of the Snowdonia range run dry.

Where the A5 London-to-Holyhead road crosses the river for the first time, just below the confluence with the Afon Merddwr, the gorges begin. Easy at first, it gradually increases in difficulty and depth as the river cuts its way downwards towards the sea. Although the road parallels the river for much of this section the steeply wooded banks and rocky cliffs limit the access and it remains hidden from the view of the passing motorists. For this reason a descent of the Conwy is a perfect means of escape from the busy world above, a descent into a river-world where the impact of man has had little effect on the surrounding environment and through which it is only possible to travel by canoe.

The Afon Conwy is not only popular for its scenery but also for the variety of sections suitable for whitewater canoeists of differing abilities. It can provide classic Grade 3 runs on the upper river and gives excellent Grade 5 sport through the final turbulent gorges above and below Penmachno Bridge and in the Fairy Glen. (*Note:* A short section starting from just above Penmachno Bridge to the foot of the Conwy Falls is effectively unnavigable because of the combination of excessive seriousness and awkward access.) Beyond The Fairy Glen the Conwy is joined by the Afon Lledre for a Grade 2 run down to the confluence with Afon Llugwy below Betws-y-Coed. From here the river meanders gently across flood plains with forested hills on either side before flowing into the tidal waters of Conwy Bay.

Access considerations on the Conwy and Llugwy
The upper Conwy must be recognised as having valuable and fragile eco-systems along both banks. The special care needed in relation to these areas is recognised by the Welsh Canoe Association and is part of the expected code of practice contained in access agreements. Apart from indigenous rare flora and an otter population in its course there are also two Sites of Special Scientific Interest (SSSIs), one of which coincides with a portage point. Co-operation in keeping to access agreements and access points is vital to the care and protection of the river. Full details of agreements are available from the Local Access Officers (WCA).

Note: For general location map of the Afon Conwy see page 112.

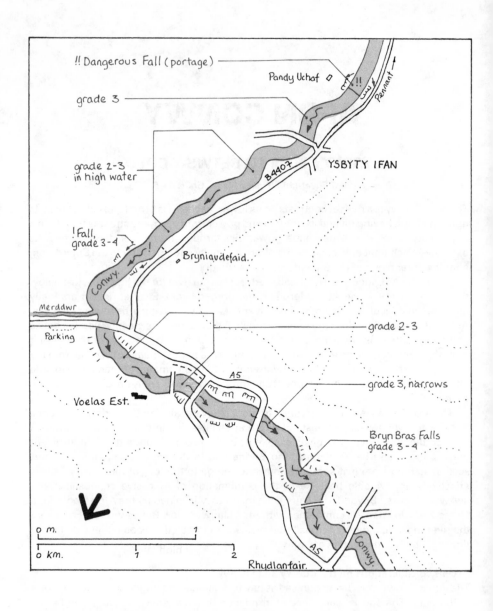

!! Dangerous Fall (portage)

Pandy Uchaf

grade 3

Pennant

YSBYTY IFAN

grade 2-3
in high water

B4407

! Fall,
grade 3-4

Conwy.

Bryniaudefaid.

Merddwr

Parking

grade 2-3

A5

grade 3, narrows

Voelas Est.

Bryn Bras Falls
grade 3-4

0 m.   1

0 km.   1   2

A5

Conwy.

Rhydlanfair.

Ysbyty Ifan to the A5

Start (842488)   Finish (856512)   Grade 3 (spate only)   Distance 2½mls/3½km

It is possible to canoe the Conwy above Ysbyty Ifan by starting below Pennant Farm (824469) half a mile up the road. The river bed is strewn with boulders and overhanging trees which become more serious as you near Pandy Uchaf. Just below Pandy Uchaf (839483) there is a dangerous fall and an awkward portage is required to avoid it. Above Ysbyty Ifan are a series of ledge drops (Grade 3 – 4) easy to inspect and portage from the left. These rapids are Ysbyty Falls and canoeists have the option of starting the run above or below them. Canoeing on this stretch is only possible after heavy rain has filled the river, otherwise you will be faced with a shallow bump and scrape the whole way down to the A5. In good water conditions the rocky bed of the river provides fast rapids (Grade 2 – 3) down to the A5 road bridge. There is a difficult section just below Bryniaudefaid Farm (855503) where the river drops into a narrow slot on the right. This can be Grade 3 – 4 depending on river levels and prior inspection is recommended in case a portage is necessary. The best exit to the A5 is upstream from the bridge on the right. There is a large layby just to the east of the bridge.

Afon Merddwr/A5 road bridge to Rhydlanfair Bridge

Start (856512)   Finish (828524)   Grade 3 (one fall, 3 – 4)   Distance 2½mls/4km

The A5 road bridge is a convenient starting point for most canoeists running the Conwy. With the additional volume of the Afon Merddwr the Conwy becomes more of a canoeable prospect in medium to low flows. From the confluence of the two rivers Grade 2 rapids carry you down past wooded banks to the Voelas estate. After a stone bridge, just beyond the buildings, the river picks up by a grade and passes under another bridge. The river is bounded here by steep rocky sides and moss-covered boulders and you are alone, for the canoe is the only reasonable means of access into this short gorge, though the A5 runs parallel to the river high above on the left.

The river passes below the A5 again at (839515) and then narrows into a fast bouncy shoot (Grade 3).

Bryn Bras Falls (Grade 3 – 4) is the next feature (836517). These can be inspected beforehand from the A5 and this is perhaps wise as a tricky right-hand route carries you into a boily hole. The calm water below gives ample room for recovery and spectating. The river broadens out for a spell with some long Grade 2 – 3 rapids, rocky in low water but bouncy in high water, before a final idle stretch of calm river brings you to Rhydlanfair Bridge, finishing an excellent Grade 3 run.

Rhydlanfair Bridge to Penmachno Bridge

Start (828524)   Finish (811534)   Grade 4 – 5   Distance 1½mls/2km

The next section is comparatively short but also sharp, with two severe drops and Grade 3 – 4 rapids, the former being extremely dangerous in spate conditions. From Rhydlanfair Bridge there are Grade 2 – 3 rapids for the first half-mile until the river rounds a right-hand bend with rock walls on the right. Here there is a Grade 5 fall (819528) as the river is split around a large central rock into two narrow channels. This fall is a serious undertaking and is run on the left-hand chute. Prior inspection and the need for safety cover is essential as there is a high probability of getting trapped. It is easy to inspect and portage on the left.

Beyond the first Grade 5 section a few Grade 3 rapids bring you to the next Grade 4 – 5 passage. Here the river descends into a narrow, twisting and boily channel before a final drop into a pool. This last drop can often produce unintentional back loops. The inspection and portage on the left are not particularly easy because of steep slippery rocks and banks. Beyond this there are a further two drops which may need inspection.

Once below these steep drops you can look back to appreciate the loss in height that the river has taken in such a short distance. In high water the first waterfall and the second section have large and dangerous stoppers and should be avoided.

A final section of Grade 3 – 4 rapids brings you quickly through this deep gorge to the Penmachno road bridge. It is important to quit the river on the left well before the bridge, below which is an horrendous and presently unnavigated cataract. Keep a wary eye out for the bridge for its grey brown stonework merges into the rock walls and is difficult to discern in poor light. Exit from the river well above the bridge and walk up to the road. As you carry your canoe over the bridge and up to the A5 and the Conwy Falls cafe, take a look downstream into the gorge and cataracts below. It is worth inspecting these cataracts *before* you make your run as a salutary reminder not to miss the 'last break-out' well before the bridge. At the cafe car-park there is a turnstile which admits tourists to the Conwy Falls.

Conwy Fall to Betws-y-Coed

Start (809535)   Finish (798546)   Grade 4 – 5 to Beaver Pool Bridge and thereafter 1 – 2
Distance 2mls/3km

The cataract below Penmachno Bridge is (at present) unnavigable and the gorge between this and the Conwy Falls can only be reached by abseil. The next section therefore effectively starts below Conwy Falls.

The Penmachno Bridge cataract leads into a rocky gorge with the Afon Machno flowing in from the left swelling the volume of the river. Just upstream on the Machno is a large waterfall observed easily from the road that crosses Pont-y-pandy by the Penmachno Woollen Mill (804528). If you cross this bridge look downstream for the old

Roman bridge. From this road there are several points where you can catch glimpses of the gorges below.

To gain the river below Conwy Falls you must scramble down from the path that starts in a layby just down the A5 from the cafe. This track was an old tollgate road on the London to Holyhead route and before that a packhorse trail.

This section of river from below Conwy Falls (known to canoeists as the Fairy Glen, though the Victorians probably only referred to the lowest section as such) is one of the finest wildwater runs in North Wales. The Conwy Falls are formed where the river splits around a large central buttress of rock upon which are the remains of an old and unsuccessful salmon ladder. The Falls themselves have been shot, though the access to

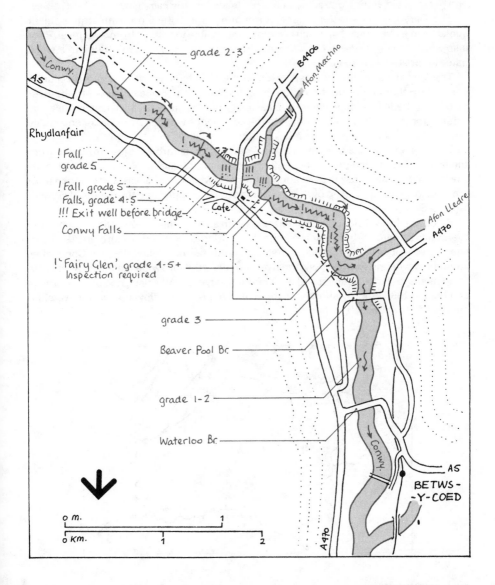

the gorge above is extremely complicated, involving abseiling. The natural amphitheatre into which the river collects soon squeezes in again to a tight gorge with numerous narrow and tricky Grade 4 – 5 rapids and falls. Discretion and common sense should prevail in assessing whether to run or portage certain drops. This section is canoeable at most water levels, however at high to spate conditions there can be river-wide stoppers with dangerous towbacks and prior inspection is essential on the day to determine whether it is safe to run the whole stretch.

Half-way down there is a brief respite as the gorge opens out and brings you to a major portage where the river is once again divided by a central rock outcrop, but this time it descends onto a chaotic boulder garden. It is easy to portage this drop on the left and get in again at the right-angle bend that leads into the Fairy Glen.

The Fairy Glen is a technical and committing Grade 4 – 5 run with large boulder chokes and a river-wide fall which is almost impossible to inspect from river level. Prior inspection can be made by following the track up from Beaver Pool Bridge to a small gate signposted 'to the Fairy Glen'.

The Welsh name for the Glen, 'Ffos-Noddyn' (ditch-chasm), is a more accurate description than the romantic Victorian name. The path also leads down to the river below the Grade 5 passages; here you can exit from the gorge or, alternatively, use it as a put-in for the Grade 3 – 4 run down to the confluence with the Afon Lledre and finally into the Beaver Pool beyond the A470 bridge.

The Beaver Pool is a brief rest for the Conwy after its turbulent journey down from the hills; however, the pool's tranquillity and stillness belies its Welsh name 'Llyn-yr-Afanc', where 'Afanc' refers to an aquatic monster which legend tells was dragged from the pool in chains and taken over Moel Siabod to be dropped into the depths of Glaslyn high on Snowdon.

Below the Beaver Pool the river eases up with a final Grade 1 – 2 section down to the Waterloo Bridge, 'Y-bont-Haearn', the iron bridge, built by Telford in 1815. An alternative exit is at the footbridge half a mile further on. Below Betws-y-Coed, after combining with the Afon Llugwy, the river broadens out into wide meanders across the flood plains towards Llanwrst and under Pont Fawr, the bridge designed by Inigo Jones and built in 1636. Shortly afterwards the river becomes tidal, flowing past the watchful guard of Conwy Castle and out into Conwy Bay.

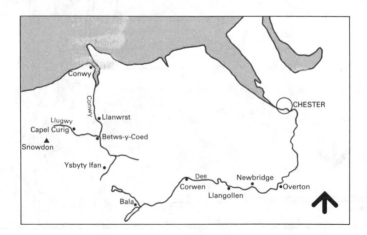

AFON LLUGWY

HELYG TO BETWS-Y-COED

OS Sheet.115   8 miles/14km   Grade 3 – 4 (some portage)

The Afon Llugwy is one of Snowdonia's most popular canoeing rivers. It rises in the southern end of the Ogwen Valley, with its source beginning at Ffynnon Llugwy reservoir below the rocky ridge of Craig yr Ysfa. Its volume is swollen by the mountain streams that run off from the Carnedds and the Glyders and at Capel Curig it is joined by the Nant Gwryd flowing out from Llynnau Mymbyr. Its combination of pleasant rapids of medium difficulty, interspersed with demanding (and at times outrageous) falls to run or portage, gives ample scope for excursions for both the competent and the expert canoeist. The outstanding beauty of the River Llugwy inspired a generation of Victorian artists who flocked to Betws-y-Coed to paint romantic scenes of woodlands and waterfalls. Since then little has changed and the river and its falls still attract the tourists today.

The Llugwy runs swiftly down from the hills and fills and drains quickly after rain. It is best to paddle it shortly after heavy rain, or even during it when you may find the river level rising as you make your descent. I have often arrived to find the river at a low level only to be told that the water had been as high as the car-park at the Snowdonia cafe the day before. This, infuriatingly, often occurs just before the weekend! A good indication of the river level can be gained by an inspection of Cobden's Falls opposite Cobden's Hotel. If there is enough water running over the central slab to make a descent then there is enough water for a good paddle. The more water, the wilder the river gets in its lower reaches.

AFON LLUGWY: STAGE 1

Upper Llugwy: Helyg to Capel Curig

Start (691601)   Finish (718580)   Grade 3 – 4 (one 5 fall)   Distance 3mls/5km

The Llugwy can be navigated from above Capel Curig. Although a small stream at Helyg it begins to increase in volume and gradient as other streams join it. This section is only possible after heavy rain and a drive up the A5 towards Ogwen Valley will enable you to view most of the river and to choose a convenient starting point close to the road. This is a narrow and boulder strewn run which builds up to Grade 3 – 4 rapids as you approach Capel Curig.

At Capel Curig, behind Joe Brown's climbing shop, is a Grade 5 fall (721582). Brown's Fall can be inspected or portaged on the right and is easy to reach via the bridge behind the climbing shop. Beyond this the Llugwy joins the Nant Gwryd which flows out of Llynnau Mymbyr.

Capel Curig to The Ugly House

Start (716577) *Finish (756575)* *Grade 3 (one 4 fall and one portage)* *Distance 3mls/5km*

This section is one of the most popular on the river and is used frequently by the outdoor centres in the area. Canoeists can start at Plas-y-Brenin, the National Centre for Mountain Activities. There is a footpath by the side of the centre that leads down to the eastern end of Lynnau Mymbyr. From here it is calm water until the confluence with the

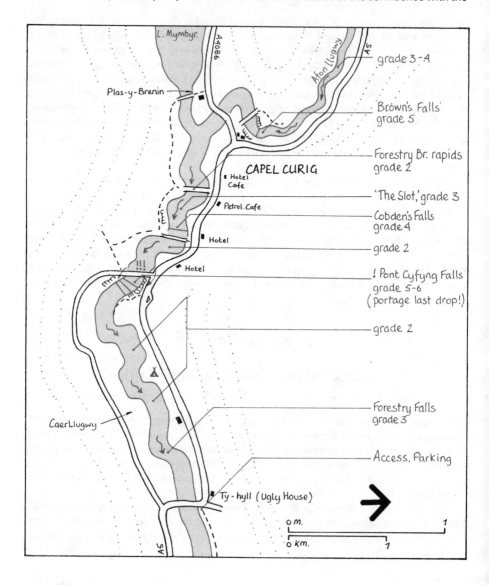

Llugwy. Small rapids follow to the Forestry Bridge (726578) which is also a convenient starting point. Grade 2 rapids begin the build-up towards Cobden's Falls with a Grade 3 slot to negotiate where the river narrows into an obvious chute.

Cobden's Falls, Grade 4 (731576), can be easily inspected beforehand either from the paths on the right-hand bank or from the footbridge opposite Cobden's Hotel. The obvious route is usually over the central slab of rock. In high water these falls can be Grade 5 with a severe stopper (portage if necessary on the right) which has been known to back-loop fourteen-foot inflatable rafts. An easier section of rapids leads down towards Pont Cyfyng (734572). This old narrow bridge used to carry the mail coaches on the Holyhead-to-London road in the last century. One of these coaches is on view opposite the Tyn-y-coed Hotel just upstream of the bridge.

At Pont Cyfyng the river narrows into twisting chutes under the bridge before cascading over a severe three-tier fall. It is easy to stop above these falls and to portage around them. For the waterfall addicts these falls can be tricky yet exciting. The first two drops are only possible in certain water conditions when they are Grade 5, and the last is not recommended (you will see why when you inspect it) and a portage must be made on the right.

Having portaged Pont Cyfyng Falls there is an exciting Grade 2 – 3 run, including Forestry Falls, a Grade 3 rapid, down to the A5 bridge at The Ugly House. At first the river meanders through a short fertile valley and there are numerous overhanging trees to watch out for. On the left you will pass the site of Caer Llugwy, a Roman fort of which little now remains but which was once a home for 5000 men. At the A5 road bridge you can exit on the left below the bridge unless you are going to continue on to Swallow Falls and the lower Llugwy.

Ty-Hyll (The Ugly House) is a curious cottage and is said to be the result of a loophole in the local law which said that if a house could be built between sunrise and sunset with smoke coming out of the chimney by dawn then the builders owned the house and the land on which it stood.

AFON LLUGWY: STAGE 3

Lower Llugwy: The Ugly House to Betws-y-Coed

Start (756575)   Finish (792567)   Grade 3 – 4 (two portages)   Distance 2½mls/4km

This section of river is often neglected but it is outstanding not only for its rapids, but also for the impressive scenery below Swallow Falls, with tall rocky outcrops above and the dense woodland on either side. From The Ugly House it is an easy run to the top of Swallow Falls. Get out on the left well above the falls and portage along the path.

Swallow Falls had been contemplated by paddlers for many years before the first descent in a kayak was finally achieved. Since then there have been many repeat descents but this type of kayaking, 'vertical rock dodging', is generally regarded as a fringe activity and most people will be quite happy to pick up their boats and move past the cataract to the river below.

After the portage past Swallow Falls you will have to descend a steep slope below the last drop to gain access to the river. A short Grade 3 – 4 rapid begins this stretch and then the river widens and runs through Grade 2 – 3 rapids. This long section builds up in pace and finally narrows into a drop with a large hole on the right, Grade 4, which can be

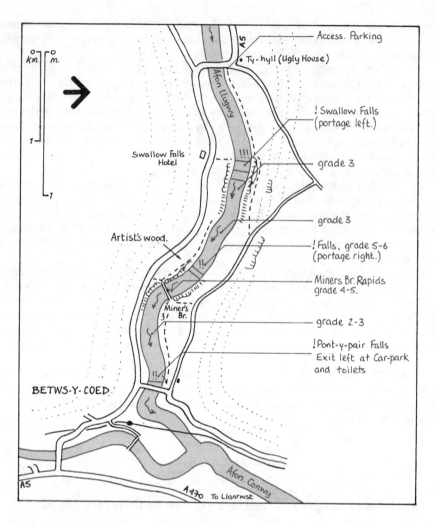

Access. Parking

A5

Ty-hyll (Ugly House)

Afon Llugwy

! Swallow Falls
(portage left.)

grade 3

Swallow Falls
Hotel

grade 3

Artist's wood.

! Falls, grade 5-6
(portage right.)

Miners Br. Rapids
grade 4-5.

Miner's
Br.

grade 2-3

! Pont-y-pair Falls
Exit left at Car-park
and toilets

BETWS-Y-COED

A5

Afon Conwy

A470 To Llanrwst

powerful in high water; inspection may be necessary. Just beyond this there are some large drops where the river flows into and under boulders (Grade 5 – 6+) and which can be portaged on the right.

It is possible to seal launch into the river just above Miners' Bridge (780569) to run the narrow and exciting channel (Grade 4 – 5) down to and under Miners' Bridge. This bridge was built to provide a short cut for miners living in Pentre-du who worked in the lead mines on the plateau to the north. The bridge is now part of a walk through Artists' Wood, so named after the many Victorian artists who visited the area, inspired by its natural beauty and scenery.

From Miners' Bridge to Betws-y-Coed are some entertaining Grade 2 – 3 rapids. The trip finishes by the car-park on the left just above Pont-y-pair Falls. These have been run (Grade 5 – 6) but most people are happy to stop above and retire to the gear shops and cafes of Betws-y-Coed for a well-earned rest. Below the bridge the river calms down and finally mingles with the waters of the Conwy as it flows towards the sea.

TOURING RIVERS

With the exception of the Tryweryn, all the rivers mentioned so far have been free-flowing rivers. There are however many other opportunities for canoeing in Britain, some of which are more convenient to the large conurbations than the fourteen rivers already described. There is also unlimited potential for canoeing on the extensive network of inland waterways, and membership of the BCU includes a free British Waterways Board licence which covers the majority of the canal system. Other major rivers have also become navigable through commercial usage and these will require a separate licence. Although developed for commercial use these waterways often pass through areas of quite attractive countryside.

In this final section of the book I have given only brief summaries for some of the more popular canoe touring rivers in Britain, to which can be added the more placid stretches of the rivers already described. Canoe touring can be anything from an afternoon paddle to a multi-day expedition with camping equipment, the latter being a particularly pleasurable way of enjoying the sport.

For further information on canoe touring and canoeing in your own area contact your local canoe club or the Touring and Recreation Committee of the British Canoe Union.

RIVER TWEED

Peebles to Berwick
Distance 70 miles/113km

The River Tweed has its source in the Tweedsmuir Hills of southern Scotland and runs eastwards from the Southern Uplands to join the North Sea at Berwick.

This is an ideal river for the touring canoeist in either kayak or open canoe. The starting point depends upon river levels. It may be possible to start upstream of Peebles in higher river levels but summer conditions may dictate a lower start to avoid unnecessary shallows.

In its upper half the river follows a deep valley which opens up into undulating countryside in the vicinity of Melrose and provides pleasant and scenic canoeing for most of its length. There are frequent Grade 1 rapids and two notable sections of Grade 2 – 3 at Fairnilee and Makerstoun, which can be easily portaged if necessary. The last sixteen miles from Coldstream to Berwick, where the river is the border between Scotland and England, can be slow, with the final five miles being tidal. There are several tributaries of the Tweed which can be canoed in reasonable water levels. An interesting section of Grade 3 – 4 whitewater can be found on the River Ettrick above Ettrick Bridge. The Tweed, like the Tay and the Spey, is also a popular fishing river and due consideration should be given to the anglers. *Note:* For general location map of the River Tweed see page 13.

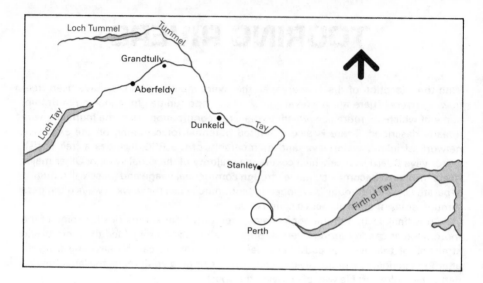

RIVER TAY

Loch Tay to Perth
Distance 47 miles/76km

The River Tay rises on the northern slopes of Ben Lui to the south-west of Tyndrum and travels nearly 120 miles from its source to the sea at Dundee. The Tay's large catchment area provides many canoeable tributaries for the whitewater enthusiast: Dochart, Ericht, Garry, Lyon and Tummel. For the canoe tourer the journey can start at the western end of Loch Tay, a long ribbon lake of fifteen miles. From its outflow at the eastern end down to Perth the canoeing is generally easy but also impressively scenic. There are, however, two sections of note. At Grandtully there is a Grade 3 – 4 section used for slalom competition and river racing and at Stanley there is a Grade 3 run from Campsie Linn to Thistlebrig including a large weir which needs inspection. The Tay is also a popular fishing river and due consideration should be shown in the fishing season to avoid disturbing the anglers or fishing pools.

RIVER TRENT

Great Haywood to Newark

Distance 80 miles/129km

The Trent is one of Britain's longest rivers and is also a major navigation. From the Staffordshire potteries the Trent runs through pleasant countryside and is at its best where it flows close to the hills that fringe it. Canoeing is possible from fairly high up depending on river levels; however, a normal starting point for touring trips is at Great Haywood, just east of Stafford. There are a number of weirs on this upper section, some of which can be run. Below the confluence with the Dove at Burton the river is wider and the weirs higher and unshootable. No permit is required for this part of the navigation. From Nottingham to Newark the Trent runs through pleasant but flat countryside with large mechanical locks. A ruined castle rises from the waterside near Newark town lock.

It is worth noting that at Holmesluice, just outside Nottingham, there is the National Watersport Centre of Holme Pierrepont with a regatta course for racing and an artificial slalom course. A fee is payable for use of the course, but public use at weekends is somewhat restricted by competitions and official training sessions and it is worth checking in advance with the Centre (☎ 0602 821212) or at Current Trends Canoe School (☎ 0602 818844) situated near the course.

Tributaries of the River Trent
Other canoeable tributaries of the River Trent are: the River Soar, running through pleasant countryside for some twenty-five miles from Leicester to the Trent; the River Dove, which rises near Buxton and is canoeable from Rocester Bridge, south of Ashbourne, to the confluence with the Trent at Burton; the River Derwent, flowing from its source in the Peak Moorlands and through a scenic gorge at Matlock where there is a popular canoe slalom site. From Matlock it is more than thirty miles to the Trent, with several weirs to portage.

For current access information on all these rivers contact the East Midlands Regional Access Officer of the BCU.

RIVER GREAT OUSE

Kempston/Bedford to Ely
Distance 71 miles/114km

The Great Ouse rises in Northampton and flows into the Wash below King's Lynn. In its upper reaches the river flows through undulating scenic and wooded countryside. This upper section is more attractive than the lower Great Ouse which passes through exposed fenland. From Kempston/Bedford to Earith, a distance of forty miles, a navigation exists with fifteen locks and weirs to negotiate. A further eleven miles brings you to the confluence of the River Cam and beyond this is Ely. It is not worth continuing beyond Ely as the river runs between raised banks. At Cardington, a couple of miles beyond Bedford, there is an artificial slalom course where competitions are held.

Tributaries of the Great Ouse
Other canoeable tributaries of the Great Ouse are: the River Cam, canoeable from its confluence with the Ouse up to Cambridge; the River Wissey, a scenic Norfolk river which is canoeable from Kilborough to the confluence with the Ouse near Denver Sluice; the Little Ouse, an attractive river which has navigation from Thetford; the River Thet, a tributary of the Little Ouse, which is canoeable from East Jarling to Thetford; the River Lark, attractive in its upper reaches between Bury St Edmunds and Mildenhall.

To the north of the Great Ouse is the River Nene, navigable from Northampton to Peterborough, a distance of sixty miles, with its most scenic run beginning at Irthlingborough.

A permit to cover the Nene, Ouse and its tributaries is available from the National Rivers Authority, Anglian Region, Aqua House, London Road, Peterborough PE2 8AG.

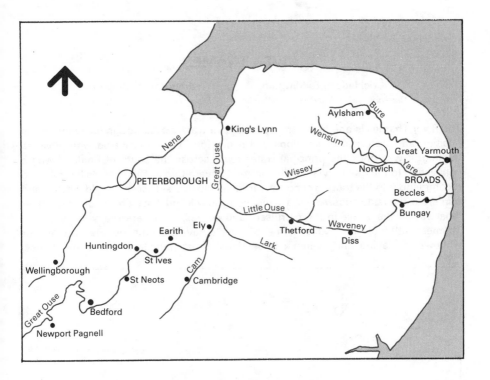

THE NORFOLK BROADS

Rivers Yare, Waveney, Bure

Although small in comparison with the connected system of Inland Waterways the Broads have long been one of Britain's most popular boating areas. The main rivers that form the Broads are situated in East Anglia between Norwich and the coast and provide well over three hundred miles of canoeable waterways. The actual broads are small shallow lakes formed by the inundation of ancient peat diggings. These waters are, for the most part, lock free although they are subject to tides. The tides, however, are virtually unnoticeable in the upper reaches of the rivers.

The River Yare runs from Norwich to Yarmouth, with pleasant scenery in its upper part and typical fenland scenery in the lower part. Norwich town centre is actually reached via the River Wensum, a tributary of the Yare.

The River Waveney, south of the Yare, has pleasant scenery and is canoeable from as far up as Diss. The Waveney joins the Yare at Breydon Water, a tidal lake that can be rough in strong winds. The river is connected to Oulton Broad, a large boating centre in the Broads.

North of the Yare is the River Bure with its tributaries, the River Ant and River Thorne. Canoeable from Aylsham, it passes through attractive broadland scenery until it meets the Yare at Great Yarmouth.

A licence is required from the Broads Authority, River Tolls Office, Thomas Harvey House, 18 Colegate, Norwich NR3 1BQ.

RIVER THAMES

Cricklade to Teddington	Teddington to Sheerness
Distance 138 miles/222km (navigation)	*Distance 66 miles/106km (tidal)*

The River Thames is one of Britain's best-known waterways through its geographical position and historical connections and it has long been associated with pleasure boating. It was once the principal water route across the south of England with a connection to the Severn via the Thames and Severn Canal. The Thames has much to recommend it to the touring canoeist – from idyllic riverside scenery, old villages and numerous riverside pubs. As it is a navigation you will find that there are plenty of other 'boaters' on the water in motorcruisers and barges. There are many locks on the Thames with adjacent weirs, some of which have become popular venues for whitewater playing and slalom competitions; most notable of these are Henley,

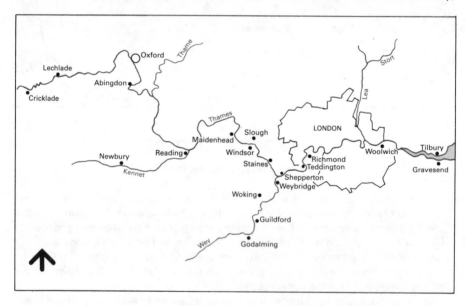

Hambleton, Marlow, Old Windsor, Bolters and Shepperton. Below Teddington the river is tidal and with an outgoing tide fast journeys can be achieved through the heart of London. The Thames is also the venue for the last leg of the annual Devizes to Westminster Canoe Race, a gruelling 24-hour marathon over 125 miles that starts on the Kennet. Other tributaries of the Thames that offer good water for touring are the Thame, the Wey and the Lea.

All pleasure craft using the Thames require a licence which may be obtained from National Rivers Authority, Thames Region, Kingsmeadow House, Kingsmeadow Road, Reading RG1 8DQ.

RIVER ARUN

Pallingham Lock to Littlehampton Harbour
Distance 22 miles/35km

Although this represents a short section of river in comparison to some of the others listed here, the Arun has much to offer the touring canoeist. It is tidal for eighteen miles from Littlehampton to Pulborough and is canoeable from Pallingham. The upper reaches are narrow and shallow and a reasonable level of water is required if this is to be attempted. From Pallingham the river flows through fields and woods which gradually open out with views of the South Downs and then through the Arundel Gap, past the town of Arundel and on to Littlehampton Harbour.

High tide at Arundel Bridge is Dover + 1hr 20mins and Littlehampton is Dover + 20mins.

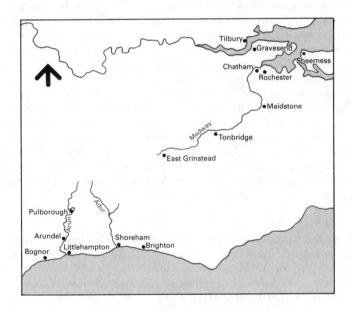

RIVER MEDWAY

Tonbridge to Allington
Distance 8 miles/29km (navigation)

Allington to Sheerness
Distance 25 miles/40km (tidal)

The Medway rises in Sussex not far from East Grinstead and flows in a north-easterly direction through Kent towards the Thames Estuary. It is possible to start some sixteen miles upstream of Tonbridge, at Ball's Green, but the river is narrow and may well be shallow in low water.

The best and most scenic section of the river is the navigation from Tonbridge to

Allington, some eight miles in length. This rural river course passes through hopfields and orchards. The tidal section of the Medway begins at Allington Lock. The banks below can be very muddy in low water and it is recommended to canoe this part of the river just after high tide. Below Rochester the river widens out into a broad estuary passing Chatham Docks and Gillingham and finally reaching the Thames Estuary at Sheerness. This last section can be busy with shipping and care should be taken with the tides to avoid being stranded on mud banks.

Licences for the Medway navigation are obtainable from the National Rivers Authority, Southern Region, Gilbourne House, Chatsworth Road, Worthing BN11 1LD.

RIVER SEVERN

Welshpool to Stourport	**Stourport to Gloucester**
Distance 84 miles/135km (free navigation)	*Distance* 43 miles/69km (canal and tidal)

The Severn is the sister river of the Wye as they both rise on the slopes of the same mountain, Plynlimon, in mid-Wales. Its long circuitous route to the sea and its gradual fall in gradient make it an ideal touring river. It is possible to canoe from Newtown although there are several weirs during the course of the river to Pool Quay, three miles north of Welshpool. From Pool Quay to Stourport an ancient right-of-navigation exists and there are many scenic stretches of river and occasional small rapids. At Ironbridge the river enters a narrow gorge and the rapids here are used as a slalom site.

Between Stourport and Gloucester the river has several locks controlled by the British Waterways Board and a licence is required (BCU membership includes BWB licence). At Tewkesbury the River Avon enters the Severn and below this the river becomes tidal. Canoeing below Gloucester is not recommended as the dangerous currents and changing channels can make navigation hazardous. Lower down, the Severn is affected by the famous Severn Bore, a spectacular series of tidal waves reaching between five and nine feet, an inspiration to both surfers and surf-canoeists.

A tributary of the River Severn
A significant tributary of the Severn is the River Teme. Flowing through pleasant surroundings it is canoeable from Ludlow, through Tenbury and eventually joins the Severn below Worcester a distance of more than forty miles. In reasonable water levels there are many small rapids to negotiate as well as several weirs. Advice on access should be obtained from the BCU or the WCA.

RIVER AVON

Alveston Mill to Tewkesbury
Distance 46 miles/74km

The River Avon is an ancient navigation and is extensively used for pleasure cruising. It is attractive throughout its length from Alveston Mill, just above Stratford, to Tewkesbury and the confluence with the Severn, a distance of forty-six miles. There are seventeen locks on this section and the river is administered by two separate bodies. Above Evesham it is the Upper Avon Navigation Trust (free to BCU members) and below Evesham it is the Lower Avon Navigation Trust. This situation originated in the eighteenth century when the two sections of river came under separate ownership. It is possible to canoe the Avon from as far up as Rugby, a further forty-four miles. However, the shallow nature of this section requires a good level of water in the river and there are several portages required. It is also heavily polluted.

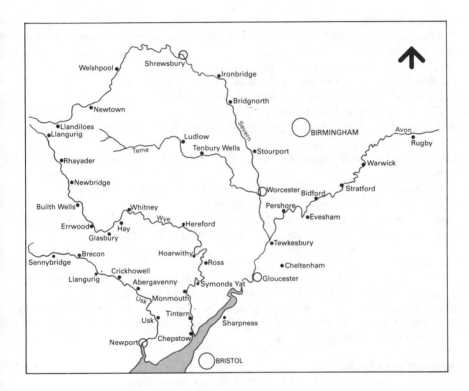

RIVER EXE AND RIVER TAMAR

These two rivers, within easy reach of the River Dart, have much to offer the touring canoeist. The Exe rises on Exmoor, and although it is generally Grade 2 its character depends upon the water level. The stretch of river between Tiverton and Exeter is the venue for the annual 'Exe Descent', a seventeen-mile canoe race during which the competitors have to negotiate several large weirs.

The Tamar, to the west, is a drowned valley similar to the Dart Estuary and has plenty to offer the canoeist. The upper non-tidal reaches of the river pass through a beautiful deep and wooded valley. Both the Exe and the Tamar are also popular rivers for fishing, and access details should be obtained from the South-West Regional Access officer of the BCU. *Note:* For general location map for Rivers Exe and Tamar see page 42.

FURTHER READING

Canoeing Techniques
The Canoeing Handbook (British Canoe Union, 1989) A guide to canoeing skills and all aspects of the sport.
Whitewater Kayaking by Ray Rowe (Salamander, 1988) A comprehensive guide to whitewater skills and techniques. Applicable to all levels of canoeing.
Placid Water Canoeing by David Train (Published privately, 1983)
A guide to flat water skills and touring.
Path of the Paddle by Bill Mason (Key Porter Books, Canada) An outstanding instructional book on open boat canoeing.
Canoe Games by Dave Ruse (A & C Black, 1986) A guide to numerous games you can play on the water.
River Rescue by Slim Ray and Les Bedchel (Appalachian Mountain Club, 1989)
An authoritative manual on river rescue techniques.
Kayak by William Nealy (Menasha Ridge Press, US, Cordee 1989) Advanced kayaking techniques presented by America's foremost canoeing cartoonist.

Magazines
Canoe Focus The official magazine of the British Canoe Union, issued free to all members.
Canoeist (S.T. and R.J. Fisher, 4 Sinodum Row, Appleford, Oxon OX14 4PE)
Britain's independent monthly canoeing magazine. Articles on all aspects of canoeing, recreation, expeditions, competitions, river guides and latest information on access, plus mail order book supplies.

Regional Canoe Guides
A Canoeist's Guide to the North-East by Nick Doll (Cicerone, 1990)
Snowdonia, Whitewater, Sea and Surf by Terry Storry (Cicerone)
Scottish Whitewater by Ian Lochead, Phill Todd (BCU/SCA)
Rivers of Cumbria by Mike Haywood (Cordee)
Guide to Scottish Rivers (SCA)
BCU Regional Guides A list of regional canoeing guides is available from the BCU.
Guide to the Waterways of the British Isles (British Canoe Union) Although dated, this contains useful background information on touring rivers, but the current access situations should be checked.

A list of guides for the UK and Europe is available from BCU Supplies or *Canoeist* magazine.

GLOSSARY

Breakout Manoeuvring the canoe out of the main flow of water into slack water. Also used to describe an eddy.

Eddy Slack water or upstream current usually behind an obstacle in the river.

Break-in Moving from slack water into the main flow.

Stopper Wave A recirculating wave caused by water flowing over an obstacle on the river bed.

Hole A stopper formed by the river flowing over and around a boulder.

Standing Wave A static wave, or hydraulic jump, caused by underwater obstacles or as the river flow meets slow or slack water.

Haystack An irregular exploding or breaking wave.

Cushion Build up of water on the upstream side of an obstacle.

Rapid Occurs when there is a drop in the gradient of the river or where the river flows over underwater obstacles.

Fall An abrupt drop in river gradient, where one is unable to see the bottom of the fall when viewed from upstream. Falls may occur in rapids.

Sweepers Fallen trees across the river, or may be partly submerged. Branches act as a trap for river debris including canoeists! The same goes for low overhanging trees.

River Right The right-hand side of the river looking downstream.

River Left The left-hand side of the river looking downstream. All references to left and right refer to river left and river right.

Buoyancy Aid A flotation jacket designed to keep you afloat and give body protection. Not to be confused with a life jacket which is designed to keep you face upwards should you lose consciousness.

Buoyancy Foam blocks or airbags; fixed in a canoe to provide floatation in the event of a capsize. Maximum buoyancy contributes to the safety of the canoe.

Helmet Canoeing crash helmet to be used on rocky or rapid rivers. Must provide adequate head protection.

Throwline, Throwbag A length of rope of at least 10 metres which is designed for fast deployment in rescue situations.

Kayak Used to describe a boat where the paddler sits down and paddles with a two bladed paddle (i.e. Eskimo Kayak).

Canoe Used to describe a craft where the paddler kneels down and uses a single bladed paddle. However in Britain we tend to call kayaks 'canoes' and canoes 'canadians'.

Playspot A particular spot on the river, a wave or stopper where you can surf waves or perform acrobatics and endos.

Endos, Enders, Popout Standing the kayak on end to the vertical position, great fun when intentional, worrying when not! A popout is when the kayak goes airborne after an endo.

Loop When a kayak cartwheels over after an ender or popout.

Capsize Turning upside down and bailing out. Remember to hang on to your kayak.

Swim What you do after bailing out of your canoe after a capsize.

Roll Righting oneself without leaving the boat after a capsize.

Support Stroke A technique to prevent a capsize.

Chicken Shoot The easiest way down a rapid, often avoiding the main flow. However, some 'chicken shoots' can be Grade 5!

Bottoming out/Vertical pin Front end of kayak getting trapped on submerged rocks after a running fall. A dangerous situation!

Siphon/Undercut Where the river flows underneath rocks.

Riparian Owner Owner, or person in possession of the right of property of the river banks.

Access Agreement An agreement between canoeists, riparian owners and anglers concerning time sharing of certain stretches of river. All access agreements should be observed by canoeists.

Trespass A wrongful act, done in disturbance of the possession of property of another, or against the person of another, against his will. Trespass can be committed by mistake or without malice, but if it is an involuntary act and inevitable accident, not arising from negligence, it is not trespass.

Bailiff A Water Authority Bailiff has powers of a constable under the Salmon and Freshwater Fisheries Act but only for enforcing that act relevant to poaching and damaging spawning beds. It is not the bailiff's job to enforce property rights of angling associations and clubs. A landowner may have his own bailiff and so may the owner of the fishing rights but they are agents of the owner acting with the authority of the person in possession. An ordinary member of an angling club does not have such authority simply by virtue of his membership.

Canoeist I would like to think that this is an environmentally aware person who takes nothing and leaves nothing as he passes down the river in search of tranquillity or excitement in idyllic surroundings.

Portage Landing before a hazard, fall or weir and carrying your canoe around it to put in below. A portage does not necessarily indicate an unnavigable stretch of river. A portage may apply to a rapid of any grading depending upon the experience or inclination of the individual at the time.

Cataract A steep rapid.

Boils Water that bubbles vertically upwards.

Current Strong flow of water in a particular direction, not necessarily downstream.

Washed-out When a rapid is smoothed out due to high water flows.

Seal launch A method of entering the water from dry land whilst in your boat.